Welcome Home
FAMILY FAVORITES

—•••—

QUICK & EASY HEALTHY*ISH* MEALS

T0198055

Hope Comerford

Photos by Bonnie Matthews

Good Books

New York, New York

Good Books books may be purchased in bulk at special discounts for sales promotion, corporate gifts, fund-raising, or educational purposes. Special editions can also be created to specifications. For details, contact the Special Sales Department, Good Books, 307 West 36th Street, 11th Floor, New York, NY 10018 or info@skyhorsepublishing.com.

Good Books is an imprint of Skyhorse Publishing, Inc.®, a Delaware corporation.

Visit our website at www.goodbooks.com.

10 9 8 7 6 5 4 3 2

Library of Congress Cataloging-in-Publication Data is available on file.

Cover design by David Ter-Avanesyan
Cover photos by Bonnie Matthews

Print ISBN: 978-1-68099-897-9
Ebook ISBN: 978-1-68099-903-7

Printed in China

Table of Contents

Welcome! ☙ 1

Breakfast ☙ 3

Main Dishes ☙ 25

Pizzas ☙ 81

Pastas ☙ 89

Salads ☙ 113

Soups, Stews & Chilies ☙ 121

Desserts ☙ 157

Metric Equivalent Measurements ☙ 186

Index ☙ 187

About the Author ☙ 196

Welcome!

Whether you like to cook on the stovetop, in the oven, with your Instant Pot, or in the slow cooker, this book has something for you! I have chosen 127 of the best family-friendly, budget-friendly, reasonably healthy, and super tasty recipes for your family, from breakfast to dessert. My hope is that these recipes will become ones your family makes memories with!

When I was a little girl, I used to stand at my meme's (grandma's) counter and watch her cook. I would pull up a chair from the kitchen table and sit on my knees so I could get in on the action. When I was very young, she started letting me stir the cookie or cake batter or sprinkle the seasoning on the pork chops. When I got a little older, she began letting me measure out the flour, sugar, butter, etc. When I was older still, she let me chop the onions, celery, carrots, etc. She rarely cooked from a recipe, but the ones she did use were well-loved and usually written in her mother's handwriting.

Over the years, I've compiled many recipes from my meme. I've gained many more from my own cooking experiences, but my favorite recipes are from her. They're the comfort food of my past! They are how my love of cooking began.

The recipes in this book are collected from home cooks across the country. They are beloved recipes from grandmas and grandpas, moms, dads, and special friends, the kind you pass from generation to generation.

As you begin journeying through this book, I always suggest reading it from cover to cover. I can't tell you the good recipes I've missed in the past by not following this advice. Don't become overwhelmed. Bookmark or dog-ear the pages of the recipes that you think your family would enjoy the most, can be made with ingredients you have around the house, or fit with their dietary needs. Then, when you've looked at everything, go back to those marked pages and narrow it down. Make a grocery list and grab what you don't already have. Voilà! You're ready to get cooking!

Your family meals are about to get easier and tastier. Now, go make those memories!

Breakfasts

Caramel Rolls

Jessalyn Wantland, Paris, TX

Makes 6–8 servings

Prep. Time: 20 minutes ⚬ *Cooking Time: 2–3 hours* ⚬ *Ideal slow-cooker size: 5-qt.*

½ cup brown sugar
½ tsp. cinnamon
½ stick (4 Tbsp.) butter
2 (8-oz.) pkg. refrigerator biscuits

1. Mix sugar and cinnamon together in a small bowl.

2. Melt butter in another small bowl.

3. Dip individual biscuits into melted butter and then into cinnamon and sugar mixture.

4. Place each covered biscuit in a greased slow cooker.

5. Cover and cook on High for 2–3 hours, or until rolls are done. Check rolls in center after 2 hours to see if they are done.

Sticky Buns

Elaine Rineer, Lancaster, PA

Makes 12 servings

Prep. Time: 20 minutes ♣ Chilling Time: 8 hours, or overnight ♣ Baking Time: 35 minutes

1 stick (8 Tbsp.) butter, *divided*
½ cup brown sugar
½ cup corn syrup
¼ cup plus 2 Tbsp. sugar
2 Tbsp. cinnamon
2 loaves frozen bread dough, thawed

1. Melt ½ stick (4 Tbsp.) of butter on stovetop or in microwave. Stir in brown sugar and corn syrup until well blended. Pour into a 9 × 13-inch baking pan.

2. Melt remaining ½ stick (4 Tbsp.) butter in microwave or on stovetop. Set aside.

3. In a small mixing bowl, combine sugar and cinnamon.

4. Break off golf-ball-sized pieces of bread dough, 12 per loaf. Dip each in melted butter and then roll in sugar-cinnamon mixture. Place coated balls in baking pan.

5. Cover and refrigerate for 8 hours, or overnight.

6. Remove from refrigerator and let stand for 30 minutes before baking.

7. Bake uncovered at 325°F for 35 minutes. Turn out of pan immediately onto serving platter.

Variation:

Add ½–¾ cup chopped pecans to mixture in pan (Step 1).

Memaw's French Toast

STOVETOP

MarJanita Martin, Batesburg, SC

Makes 2–4 servings

Prep. Time: 15 minutes ☙ Cooking Time: 14 minutes

1 cup milk
4 eggs
1 tsp. cinnamon
¼ tsp. nutmeg
½ tsp. honey
1 tsp. vanilla extract
¼ tsp. salt
Dash of pepper
4–6 slices of bread

1. Beat all ingredients, except bread, together in a large mixing bowl.

2. Preheat buttered frying pan or griddle.

3. Dip bread in the mixture and put in the pan or on the griddle. Note: Don't let bread soak long in the mixture.

4. Fry on both sides until beautifully browned.

Serving suggestion:

Top with butter, peanut butter, whipped topping, caramel, or fruit.

Note:

For crisper French toast, follow instructions. For softer French toast, pour the leftover mixture on top of the pieces of bread once placed in the pan or on the griddle.

Blueberry French Toast

Stacie Skelly, Millersville, PA

Makes 12 servings

Prep. Time: 30 minutes ⚜ *Chilling Time: 6–12 hours* ⚜ *Baking Time: 1 hour*

12–15 slices day-old bread
8-oz. pkg. cream cheese
1 cup frozen blueberries
12 eggs
2 cups milk
⅓ cup honey

Sauce:
1 cup sugar
2 Tbsp. cornstarch
1 cup water
1 cup blueberries

1. Grease 9 × 13-inch baking pan.

2. Cube bread and spread in pan.

3. Cube cream cheese. Distribute evenly over bread.

4. Sprinkle blueberries on top.

5. In a mixing bowl, blend eggs, milk, and honey.

6. Pour over pan contents.

7. Cover. Refrigerate 6–8 hours, or overnight.

8. Remove from refrigerator 30 minutes before baking.

9. Bake, covered, at 350°F for 30 minutes.

10. Uncover. Bake 30 more minutes.

11. To make the sauce, mix sugar, cornstarch, and water in a saucepan. Bring to a boil. Stir in blueberries. Reduce heat, cooking until blueberries burst.

12. Serve sauce warm over French toast.

Baked Oatmeal

Lena Sheaffer, Port Matilda, PA
Susie Nissley, Millersburg, OH
Esther Nafziger, Bluffton, OH
Katie Stoltzfus, Leola, PA
Martha Hershey, Ronks, PA
Annabelle Unternahrer, Shipshewana, IN

Makes 4–6 servings

Prep. Time: 10 minutes ♣ Baking Time: 30 minutes

½ cup oil

I cup honey or brown sugar

2 eggs

3 cups rolled or quick oats, uncooked

2 tsp. baking powder

I cup milk

½ tsp. cinnamon or nutmeg, *optional*

I cup chopped nuts, raisins, apples, or other fruit*

1. Combine oil, honey or brown sugar, and eggs in a large mixing bowl.

2. Add dry oats, baking powder, and milk. Add spice if using. Mix well.

3. Add nuts and/or fruit. Mix well.

4. Pour into a greased 8-inch-square baking pan.

5. Bake at 350°F for 30 minutes.

6. Serve hot, cold, or at room temperature with milk.

---

* Add any or all of these: ½ cup dried cherries, ½ cup dried cranberries, ½ cup cut-up apricots.

Sunrise Baked Oatmeal

MarJanita Martin, Batesburg, SC

Makes 6–7 servings

*Prep. Time: 15 minutes   *   *Baking Time: 25–30 minutes*

¾ cup oil
1¼ cups sugar
4 eggs
1 Tbsp. baking powder
¾ tsp. salt
1 Tbsp. vanilla extract
1½ Tbsp. cinnamon
2 cups milk
6 cups quick oats
½ cup brown sugar
3 Tbsp. honey
3 Tbsp. maple syrup

1. Mix oil and sugar together well in a large bowl.

2. Add eggs and mix until creamy.

3. Add baking powder, salt, vanilla, cinnamon, and milk.

4. Stir in oats.

5. Pour into greased 9 × 13-inch dish.

6. Top with the brown sugar, honey, and maple syrup.

7. Bake at 350°F for 25–30 minutes.

Serving suggestion:

Goes well with milk and fruit. It also tastes great in yogurt parfaits, instead of granola.

Easter-Morning Breakfast Casserole

MarJanita Martin, Batesburg, SC

Makes 10–12 servings

Prep. Time: 30 minutes & Refrigeration Time: 8 hours
Baking Time: 50 minutes & Setting Time: 10 minutes

6 eggs
2 cups milk
6 slices bread, cubed
1 tsp. salt
1 tsp. mustard
1 lb. sausage, browned
3 slices bacon, cooked and chopped
1 cup shredded cheese
4-oz. can mushrooms, drained
1 small onion, chopped
1 small green pepper, chopped
1 tsp. Worcestershire sauce
2 sticks (1 cup) butter
2 cups crispy rice cereal

1. Mix all ingredients, except the crispy rice cereal and butter, together in a large bowl.

2. Pour into a greased 9 × 13-inch dish.

3. Refrigerate at least 8 hours before baking.

4. After refrigeration, bake at 350°F for 30 minutes.

5. Meanwhile, melt butter in a saucepan and stir in the cereal until mixed.

6. Remove from heat.

7. When the 30-minute bake time is up, pour the butter/cereal mixture over the casserole.

8. Return the casserole to the oven, and bake for another 20 minutes.

9. Allow to set 10 minutes before serving.

Tip:

This would be a great casserole for the family to assemble together on a Saturday night and bake Sunday morning!

Overnight Breakfast Casserole

Hannah D. Burkholder, Bridgewater, VA
Esther S. Martin, Ephrata, PA

Makes 8–10 servings

Prep. Time: 45 minutes ❦ Chilling Time: 8 hours, or overnight ❦ Baking Time: 1 hour

1 lb. fresh bulk sausage
4 cups cubed day-old bread
2 cups shredded sharp cheddar cheese
1 tsp. dry mustard
10 eggs, slightly beaten
4 cups milk
1 tsp. salt
Freshly ground pepper to taste
¼ cup chopped or grated onion
½ cup peeled, chopped tomatoes, *optional*
½ cup diced green and red peppers, *optional*
½ cup sliced fresh mushrooms, *optional*

1. Cook the sausage in a skillet until browned. Drain and break up the meat into small pieces. Set aside.

2. Place bread in buttered 9 × 13-inch baking dish. Sprinkle with cheese.

3. Combine the next six ingredients. Pour evenly over the bread and cheese.

4. Sprinkle cooked sausage and chopped tomatoes, peppers, and mushrooms (if using) over the top.

5. Cover and chill in refrigerator for 8 hours, or overnight.

6. Preheat oven to 325°F. Bake uncovered for 1 hour. Tent with foil if top begins to brown too quickly.

Country Brunch

Esther J. Mast, Lancaster, PA
Barbara Yoder, Christiana, PA
Ruth Ann Gingrich, New Holland, PA
Lafaye Musser, Denver, PA

Makes 12–15 servings

Prep. Time: 30 minutes & Chilling Time: 8 hours, or overnight
Baking Time: 45–60 minutes & Standing Time: 10–15 minutes

16 slices firm white bread

1⅔–2 lb. (2½ cups) cubed ham or browned sausage, drained

1 lb. (3 cups) shredded cheddar cheese

1 lb. (3 cups) shredded mozzarella cheese

8 eggs, beaten

3½ cups milk

½ tsp. dry mustard

¼ tsp. onion powder

½ tsp. seasoning salt

1 Tbsp. parsley

Topping:

3 cups uncrushed cornflakes

1 stick (8 Tbsp.) butter, melted

1. Trim crusts from bread and cut slices in half.

2. Grease a 10 × 15-inch baking dish.

3. Layer ingredients in this order: cover bottom of pan with half the bread, top with half the ham, then half the cheddar cheese, and then half the mozzarella cheese.

4. Repeat layers once more.

5. In large mixing bowl, combine eggs, milk, dry mustard, onion powder, seasoning salt, and parsley. Mix well and pour over layers.

6. Cover and refrigerate for 8 hours, or overnight.

7. Remove from refrigerator 30 minutes before baking.

8. Combine cornflakes and butter and sprinkle over casserole.

9. Cover loosely with foil to prevent over-browning. Bake at 375°F for 45 minutes.

10. Remove from oven and let stand 10–15 minutes before cutting into squares.

Fiesta Hashbrowns

Dena Mell-Dorchy, Royal Oak, MI

Makes 8 servings

Prep. Time: 15 minutes ⚜ *Cooking Time: 8–9 hours* ⚜ *Ideal slow-cooker size: 3- or 4-qt.*

1 lb. ground turkey sausage
½ cup chopped onion
5 cups frozen diced hash browns
8 oz. low sodium chicken stock
1 small red sweet pepper, diced
1 jalapeño, seeded and finely diced
1½ cups sliced mushrooms
2 Tbsp. quick-cooking tapioca
½ cup shredded Monterey Jack cheese

1. Spray slow cooker with nonstick spray.

2. In a large skillet, brown sausage and onion over medium heat. Drain off fat.

3. Combine sausage mixture, hash browns, chicken stock, sweet pepper, jalapeño, mushrooms, and quick-cooking tapioca in cooker; stir to combine.

4. Cover and cook on Low for 8–9 hours. Stir before serving. Top with shredded Monterey Jack cheese.

Italian Sausage and Sweet Pepper Hash

Hope Comerford, Clinton Township, MI

Makes 6–8 servings

Prep. Time: 10 minutes ❧ *Cooking Time: 6½ hours* ❧ *Ideal slow-cooker size: 4-qt.*

12-oz. pkg. Italian turkey sausage, cut lengthwise, then into ½-inch pieces

16 oz. frozen diced potatoes

1½ cups sliced sweet onion

1 yellow pepper, sliced

1 green pepper, sliced

1 red pepper, sliced

¼ cup melted butter

1 tsp. sea salt

½ tsp. pepper

½ tsp. dried thyme

½ tsp. dried parsley

½ cup shredded Swiss cheese

1. Spray crock with nonstick spray.

2. Place sausage, frozen potatoes, onion, and sliced peppers into crock.

3. Mix melted butter with salt, pepper, thyme, and parsley. Pour over contents of crock and stir.

4. Cover and cook on Low for 6 hours. Sprinkle with the Swiss cheese, then cover and cook for an additional 20 minutes, or until the cheese is melted.

Breakfast Pizza

Jessica Hontz, Coatesville, PA

Makes 8 servings

Prep. Time: 10 minutes & Baking Time: 20–25 minutes

10-oz. refrigerated pizza crust

8 eggs

¼ cup milk or cream

6 slices bacon, cooked crisp and crumbled

2 cups shredded cheddar, or Monterey Jack, cheese

1. Unroll pizza crust onto baking sheet.

2. Bake at 425°F for 10 minutes.

3. Whisk together eggs and milk in a large mixing bowl.

4. Cook in skillet until eggs start to congeal, about 3–4 minutes. Spoon onto crust.

5. Top with bacon and cheese.

6. Bake an additional 10 minutes until eggs are set and crust is golden brown.

Turkey Bacon, Spinach, and Gruyère Quiche

Hope Comerford, Clinton Township, MI

Makes 4–6 servings

Prep. Time: 15 minutes ☙ Cooking Time: 3–4 hours ☙ Ideal slow-cooker size: 6-qt.

8 eggs

I cup unsweetened almond milk

I tsp. salt

I tsp. pepper

I tsp. garlic powder

I tsp. onion powder

½ cup chopped onion

5 slices turkey bacon, diced

2 handfuls (about 2 oz.) fresh spinach leaves

8 oz. Gruyère cheese, shredded

1. In a bowl, mix the eggs, milk, salt, pepper, garlic powder, and onion powder. Pour this into the bottom of your greased crock.

2. Sprinkle the onion and bacon evenly over the surface of the eggs.

3. Spread the spinach all over the top of the egg mixture in your crock.

4. Cover the spinach with the shredded cheese.

5. Cover and cook on Low for 3–4 hours, or until it is completely set in the middle.

Huevos Rancheros in Crock

SLOW COOKER

Pat Bishop, Bedminster, PA

Makes 6 servings

Prep. Time: 25 minutes & Cooking Time: 2 hours & Ideal slow-cooker size: 6-qt.

3 cups gluten-free salsa, room temperature

2 cups cooked beans, drained, room temperature

6 eggs, room temperature

Salt and pepper to taste

⅓ cup grated Mexican-blend cheese, *optional*

6 white corn tortillas, for serving

1. Mix salsa and beans in slow cooker.

2. Cook on High for 1 hour or until steaming.

3. With a spoon, make 6 evenly spaced dents in the salsa mixture; try not to expose the bottom of the crock. Break an egg into each dent.

4. Salt and pepper eggs. Sprinkle with cheese if you wish.

5. Cover and continue to cook on High until egg whites are set and yolks are as firm as you like them, approximately 20–40 minutes.

6. To serve, scoop out an egg with some beans and salsa. Serve with warm tortillas.

Italian Frittata

Hope Comerford, Clinton Township, MI

Makes 6 servings

Prep. Time: 10 minutes ❧ *Cooking Time: 3–4 hours* ❧ *Ideal slow-cooker size: 5- or 6-qt.*

10 eggs
1 Tbsp. chopped fresh basil
1 Tbsp. chopped fresh mint
1 Tbsp. chopped fresh sage
1 Tbsp. chopped fresh oregano
½ tsp. sea salt
⅛ tsp. pepper
1 Tbsp. grated Parmesan cheese
¼ cup diced prosciutto
½ cup chopped onion

1. Spray your crock with nonstick spray.

2. In a bowl, mix the eggs, basil, mint, sage, oregano, sea salt, pepper, and Parmesan. Pour this mixture into the crock.

3. Sprinkle the prosciutto and onion evenly over the egg mixture in the crock.

4. Cover and cook on Low for 3–4 hours.

Main Dishes

Hearty Pot Roast

Colleen Heatwole, Burton, MI

Makes 12 servings, about 1 cup per serving

Prep. Time: 30 minutes ⚘ *Roasting Time: 2–2½ hours* ⚘ *Standing Time: 10 minutes*

4-lb. beef roast, ideally rump roast
4 medium red potatoes, cut in thirds
3 medium carrots, quartered
2 ribs celery, chopped
2 medium onions, sliced
½ cup flour
6-oz. can tomato paste
¼ cup water
I tsp. instant beef bouillon, or I beef bouillon cube
¼ tsp. pepper

1. Place roast in 9 × 13-inch baking pan or roaster.

2. Arrange vegetables around roast.

3. Combine flour, tomato paste, water, bouillon, and pepper in small bowl.

4. Pour over meat and vegetables.

5. Cover. Roast at 325°F for 2–2½ hours, or until meat thermometer registers 170°F.

6. Allow meat to stand for 10 minutes.

7. Slice and place on platter surrounded by vegetables.

8. Pour gravy over top. Place additional gravy in bowl and serve along with platter.

Variation:

You can make this in a large oven cooking bag. Combine flour, tomato paste, water, bouillon, and pepper in a bowl. Pour into cooking bag. Place in 9 × 13-inch baking pan. Add roast to bag in pan. Add vegetables around roast in bag. Close bag with its tie. Make six 1/2-inch slits on top of bag. Roast according to instructions in Step 5 and following.

Salsa Verde Pork

SLOW COOKER

Hope Comerford, Clinton Township, MI

Makes 6 servings

Prep. Time: 20 minutes & Cooking Time: 6–6½ hours & Ideal slow-cooker size: 4-qt.

1½-lb. boneless pork loin

1 large sweet onion, halved and sliced

2 large tomatoes, chopped

16-oz. jar gluten-free salsa verde (green salsa)

½ cup dry white wine

4 cloves garlic, minced

1 tsp. cumin

½ tsp. chili powder

1. Place the pork loin in the crock and add the rest of the ingredients on top.

2. Cover and cook on Low for 6–6½ hours.

3. Break apart the pork with two forks and mix with contents of crock.

Serving suggestion:

Serve over cooked brown rice or quinoa.

Smoky Brisket

Angeline Lang, Greeley, CO

Makes 8–10 servings

Prep. Time: 5 minutes   Cooking Time: 10–12 hours   Ideal slow-cooker size: 4½- to 5-qt.

2 medium onions, sliced
3–4-lb. beef brisket
1 Tbsp. smoke-flavored salt
1 tsp. celery seed
1 Tbsp. mustard seed
½ tsp. pepper
12-oz. bottle chili sauce

1. Arrange onions in bottom of slow cooker.

2. Sprinkle both sides of meat with smoke-flavored salt.

3. Combine celery seed, mustard seed, pepper, and chili sauce. Pour over meat.

4. Cover. Cook on Low 10–12 hours.

Pork Chop Pizziola

Rose-Marie Vieira, ND

Makes 2–4 servings

Prep. Time: 5 minutes & *Cooking Time: 30 minutes*

3 Tbsp. olive oil

1 Tbsp. butter

2–4 cloves garlic, chopped, or ¼–½ tsp. garlic powder

1 medium onion, chopped, *optional*

1 Tbsp. Italian seasoning

Salt and pepper to taste

2–4 medium-sized pork chops

24-oz. jar of your favorite spaghetti sauce

½ cup sliced pepperoni, *divided*

2¼-oz. can sliced olives

1–2 cups Mexican shredded cheese

½ cup pepperoncini, *optional*

1. Heat up the olive oil in electric skillet set to 350°F, or a large nonstick pan.

2. Drop in the butter to melt.

3. Add garlic and onion; cook until translucent.

4. Sprinkle in seasonings; stir and cook until fragrant.

5. In separate pan, preferably cast iron, sear the pork chops, cooking until mostly done.

6. Transfer to electric skillet.

7. Add spaghetti sauce. Stir all together, heating well.

9. Lay down half of the sliced pepperoni across the top.

10. Sprinkle the sliced olives evenly on top.

11. Spread the cheese evenly on top.

12. Top with pepperoncini, if using, distributing evenly.

13. Cover with lid of electric skillet, or heavy duty foil. You want to create steam to melt the cheese. Heat for about 10 minutes, until cheese melts.

Serving suggestion:
Serve with some hot garlic bread.

Main Dishes 🌿 **33**

Cranberry-Apple Stuffed Pork Loin

Hope Comerford, Clinton Township, MI

Makes 4–6 servings

Prep. Time: 20 minutes & Cook Time: 30 minutes

3-lb. pork tenderloin

2 Tbsp. Dijon mustard

1 Tbsp. brown sugar

1 cup diced apple (skins removed)

½ cup dried cranberries

1½ tsp. sea salt, *divided*

¼ tsp. pepper, *divided*

1 tsp. garlic powder

1 tsp. onion powder

½ tsp. dried rosemary

¼ tsp. dried sage

3 Tbsp. olive oil, *divided*

2 medium onions, peeled and chopped into thick segments

1 cup chicken broth

1. Butterfly the tenderloin and pound it so that it is evenly thick across.

2. In a small bowl, mix the Dijon mustard and brown sugar. Spread this over the tenderloin.

3. In another bowl, mix the diced apple and cranberries with ¼ teaspoon of sea salt and ⅛ teaspoon of pepper. Spread it over the tenderloin, staying about ½ inch from the edges.

4. Roll the tenderloin as tightly as possible and tie in several places with cooking twine.

5. Mix the remaining sea salt, the garlic powder, the onion powder, the rosemary, the sage, and the remaining pepper and pat it onto the tenderloin, covering it on all sides.

6. Set the Instant Pot to the Sauté function and pour in 1½ tablespoons olive oil to heat.

7. When the oil is hot, carefully sear the tenderloin on all sides. This will take 5 to 10 minutes. Remove the pork loin and set aside.

8. Pour in the remaining olive oil and add the onions. Cook for about 4 minutes, or until slightly translucent.

9. Pour in the broth and scrape the bottom of the pot with a wooden spoon or spatula to deglaze. Press Cancel.

10. Place the tenderloin on top of the onion.

11. Secure the lid and set the vent to sealing. Set the cook time for 30 minutes on the Meat setting.

12. When the cook time is over, let the pressure release naturally.

Instant Pot Boneless Short Ribs

Hope Comerford, Clinton Township, MI

Makes 4 servings

Prep. Time: 20 minutes ✣ Cook Time: 53–55 minutes

1 ½ Tbsp. olive oil

3 lb. boneless short ribs

½ tsp. salt

⅛ tsp. pepper

1 large onion, sliced

6 cloves garlic, smashed

1 cup beef stock

¼ cup balsamic vinegar

¾ cup red wine

4 carrots, cut into 2-inch chunks

Sprig rosemary

Sprig thyme

2 Tbsp. cold water

2 Tbsp. cornstarch

Serving suggestion:
Serve with mashed or baked potatoes.

1. Set the Instant Pot to the Sauté function and pour in the olive oil.

2. Sprinkle the short ribs with the salt and pepper, then brown them on all sides in the inner pot. Do this in batches if necessary. Set them aside.

3. Add the onion and garlic to the inner pot and sauté for 3–5 minutes.

4. Pour the beef stock into the inner pot and scrape the bottom to remove any bits that may be stuck. Press Cancel.

5. Place the short ribs back into the inner pot, along with the balsamic vinegar, red wine, carrots, rosemary, and thyme.

6. Secure the lid and set the vent to sealing. Manually set the cook time for 50 minutes on high pressure.

7. When the cook time is over, let the pressure release naturally for 20 minutes, then release the remaining pressure manually.

8. Switch the Instant Pot to the Sauté function.

9. Mix the cold water and cornstarch. Gently stir this mixture into the contents of the inner pot and let simmer until the sauce is thickened a bit, about 3 to 5 minutes.

10. Serve the short ribs and carrots with the sauce spooned over the top.

Mom's Beer Ribs

Kristene Hanson, O'Fallon, IL

Makes 4–6 servings

Prep. Time: 15 minutes ❧ *Cooking Time: 8 hours* ❧ *Ideal slow-cooker size: 6-qt.*

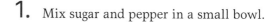

1 cup sugar

4 Tbsp. pepper

Family-size pack of boneless country style pork ribs (you can use bone-in as well)

1–3 Tbsp. cooking oil

1–2 large onions

1 bunch cilantro

12-oz. can of beer

1. Mix sugar and pepper in a small bowl.

2. Rub each side of the ribs with the sugar and pepper mixture.

3. In a frying pan, heat the oil until it is hot.

4. Place 2 or 3 ribs in and just brown the outside of each side for a minute or two, or until it has a nice crispy brown texture. Continue doing this with all the ribs. Remove and place along the bottom of the crock. (You can fry up as many of the ribs as you want at a time, but try to not overcrowd them so they get a nice crispy brown crust.)

5. Cut onion into large strips and place on top and in between the ribs in the crock.

6. Wash cilantro and break or cut into small pieces, throwing the stems away.

7. Sprinkle cilantro on top of onions and ribs in the crock.

8. Pour the can of beer over the top of ribs, onion, and cilantro.

9. Cover and cook on Low for 8 hours.

Barbecued Spareribs

Jane Geigley, Lancaster, PA

Makes 3–4 servings

Prep. Time: 15 minutes ⚘ *Baking Time: 3–4 hours* ⚘ *Grilling or Roasting Time: 30 minutes*

3 lb. spareribs

Sauce:

½ cup chopped onion

2 Tbsp. butter

2 (10½-oz.) cans tomato soup

1 tsp. hot sauce

1 Tbsp. vinegar

1 cup brown sugar

⅓ cup Worcestershire sauce

¼ tsp. ground cloves

1. Lay ribs in a single layer in a roaster or on a baking sheet with sides. Cover.

2. Bake at 300°F for 3–3½ hours, or until meat is fall-off-the-bones tender.

3. Meanwhile, in medium-sized saucepan, cook onion in butter until tender.

4. Stir in soup, hot sauce, vinegar, brown sugar, Worcestershire sauce, and cloves.

5. Simmer, uncovered, 5 minutes, stirring often.

6. Continue roasting ribs, uncovered, in oven, or move to grill.

7. Brush with sauce and roast or grill 5 minutes.

8. Turn ribs over and brush with sauce. Roast or grill 5 more minutes.

9. Turn and brush with sauce every 5 minutes for a total of 20 more minutes.

Kielbasa and Cabbage

Mary Ann Lefever, Lancaster, PA

Makes 4 servings

Prep. Time: 10–15 minutes & *Cooking Time: 3-4 hours* & *Ideal slow-cooker size: 4- or 5-qt.*

I lb. turkey kielbasa, cut into 4 chunks

4 large white potatoes, cut into chunks

I-lb. head green cabbage, shredded

I qt. whole tomatoes (strained if you don't like seeds)

Onion, thinly sliced, *optional*

1. Layer kielbasa, then potatoes, and then cabbage into slow cooker.

2. Pour tomatoes over top.

3. Top with sliced onion if you wish.

4. Cover. Cook on High 3–4 hours, or until meat is cooked through and vegetables are as tender as you like them.

Variation:

If desired, brown kielbasa in a skillet over medium heat before adding to slow cooker.

Italian Sausage Dinner

Janessa Hochstedler, East Earl, PA

Makes 6 servings

Prep. Time: 10 minutes ⚶ *Cooking Time: 5–10 hours* ⚶ *Ideal slow-cooker size: 4-qt.*

1½ lb. Italian sausage, cut in ¾-inch slices

2 Tbsp. A.1. steak sauce

28-oz. can diced Italian-style tomatoes, with juice

2 chopped green peppers

½ tsp. red pepper flakes, *optional*

2 cups uncooked instant rice

1. Place all ingredients, except rice, in slow cooker.

2. Cover and cook on Low 7½–9½ hours, or on High 4½ hours.

3. Stir in uncooked rice. Cover and cook an additional 20 minutes on High or Low.

Chicken Baked with Red Onions, Potatoes, and Rosemary

OVEN

Kristine Stalter, Iowa City, IA

Makes 8 servings

Prep. Time: 10–15 minutes ⚭ *Baking Time: 45–60 minutes*

2 red onions, each cut into 10 wedges

1 ¼ lb. new potatoes, unpeeled and cut into chunks

2 bulbs garlic, separated into cloves, unpeeled

Salt and pepper to taste

3 tsp. extra-virgin olive oil

2 Tbsp. balsamic vinegar

Approximately 5 sprigs rosemary

8 chicken thighs, skin removed

1. Spread onions, potatoes, and garlic in single layer over bottom of large roasting pan so that they will crisp and brown.

2. Season with salt and pepper.

3. Pour over the oil and balsamic vinegar and add rosemary, leaving some sprigs whole and stripping the leaves off the rest.

4. Toss vegetables and seasonings together.

5. Tuck chicken pieces among vegetables.

6. Bake at 400°F for 45–60 minutes, or until chicken and vegetables are cooked through.

7. Transfer to a big platter, or take to the table in the roasting pan.

Barbecued Chicken Thighs

Ida H. Goering, Dayton, VA

Makes 6 servings

Prep. Time: 10 minutes   ♣   Marinating Time: 2–4 hours   ♣   Grilling Time: 15–22 minutes

6 Tbsp. apple cider vinegar
3 Tbsp. canola oil
3 Tbsp. ketchup
¼ tsp. black pepper
¼ tsp. poultry seasoning
12 boneless, skinless chicken thighs

1. Combine all ingredients except chicken thighs in a large bowl.

2. Submerge thighs in sauce in bowl.

3. Marinate 2–4 hours, stirring several times to be sure meat is well covered.

4. Grill over medium heat, turning after 10–15 minutes.

5. Grill another 5–7 minutes. Watch carefully so meat doesn't dry out. Remove from grill earlier if finished.

Baked Chicken Fingers

Lori Rohrer, Washington Boro, PA

Makes 6 servings

Prep. Time: 20 minutes & *Baking Time: 20 minutes*

1½ cups fine, dry bread crumbs

½ cup grated Parmesan cheese

1½ tsp. salt

1 Tbsp. dried thyme

1 Tbsp. dried basil

7 boneless, skinless chicken breast halves, cut into 1½-inch slices

½ cup melted butter

1. Combine bread crumbs, cheese, salt, and herbs in a shallow bowl. Mix well.

2. Dip chicken pieces in butter, and then into crumb mixture, coating well.

3. Place coated chicken on greased baking sheet in a single layer.

4. Bake at 400°F for 20 minutes.

Variations:

1. In Step 1, use 1 Tbsp. garlic powder, 1 Tbsp. chives, 2 tsp. Italian seasoning, 2 tsp. parsley, ½ tsp. onion salt, ½ tsp. pepper, and 1/4 tsp. salt (instead of 1½ tsp. salt, 1 Tbsp. thyme, and 1 Tbsp. basil).

—Ruth Miller, Wooster, OH

2. Use boneless, skinless chicken thighs, and do not cut them into slices. Bake at 350°F for 20 minutes. Turn chicken. Bake an additional 20 minutes.

—Eleanor Larson, Glen Lyon, PA

Chicken Parmesan

Jessalyn Wantland, Napoleon, OH

Makes 4 servings

Prep. Time: 10 minutes   *Baking Time: 45 minutes*

4 boneless, skinless chicken breast
halves, about 6 oz. each

I egg, beaten

¾ cup Italian-seasoned bread crumbs

25-oz. jar pasta sauce

I cup shredded Parmesan cheese

1. Grease 7 × 11-inch baking dish.

2. Place egg in shallow bowl.

3. Place bread crumbs in another shallow bowl.

4. Dip each piece of chicken in egg, and then in bread crumbs.

5. Place coated chicken in baking dish.

6. Bake at 400°F for 30 minutes.

7. Spoon pasta sauce over chicken.

8. Top evenly with cheese.

9. Bake another 15 minutes, or until heated through and cheese is melted.

Sweet and Sour Chicken

Janette Fox, Honey Brook, PA

Makes 6–8 servings

Prep. Time: 15 minutes ❧ Cooking Time: 4 hours ❧ Ideal slow-cooker size: 5-qt.

3 lb. boneless, skinless chicken thighs
½ cup chopped onion
½ green pepper, chopped
15-oz. can pineapple chunks in juice
¾ cup ketchup
¼ cup brown sugar, packed
2 Tbsp. apple cider vinegar
2 tsp. soy sauce
½ tsp. garlic salt
½ tsp. salt
¼ tsp. black pepper
Cooked rice

1. Grease interior of slow-cooker crock.

2. Put chicken in crock. If you need to add a second layer, stagger the pieces so they don't directly overlap each other.

3. Scatter onion and green pepper over top.

4. In a mixing bowl, combine pineapple chunks and juice, ketchup, brown sugar, vinegar, soy sauce, garlic salt, salt, and black pepper.

5. Spoon over chicken, onion, and green pepper.

6. Cover. Cook on Low 4 hours, or until instant read meat thermometer registers 165°F when stuck into center of thighs.

7. Serve over cooked rice.

Lancaster County Ham Balls

MarJanita Martin, Batesburg, SC

Makes 6–8 servings

Prep. Time: 30 minutes ⚥ *Cooking Time: 4 hours* ⚥ *Ideal slow-cooker size: 6–7 qt.*

Meat:

2 lb. ham loaf

2 cups bread crumbs

2 eggs, beaten

1 cup milk

1 Tbsp. garlic powder

¼ cup diced onion, *optional*

Sauce:

2 cups brown sugar

1 cup vinegar

1 cup water

1 tsp. mustard

1 Tbsp. Worcestershire sauce

1. Mix meat ingredients together and shape into balls. Tip: You can use a ¼ cup measuring cup to measure out the meat for each ham ball, or use a cookie scoop for appetizer ham balls.

2. Mix sauce ingredients together and boil 5 minutes while stirring constantly.

3. Place ham balls in greased slow cooker and pour sauce over top.

4. Cook on Low for 4–6 hours.

Serving suggestion:

We love these with rice. For eating it true Lancaster County style though, these are usually served with brown-buttered noodles.

Veggie and Beef Stir Fry

Margaret H. Moffitt, Middleton, TN

Makes 4 servings

Prep. Time: 15–20 minutes ⚬ *Cooking Time: 30–35 minutes*

¼ lb. beef tenderloin

2 tsp. olive oil

I onion, chopped coarsely

I small zucchini, chopped coarsely

3 cups coarsely chopped broccoli florets

½ small yellow squash, chopped coarsely

½ cup uncooked brown rice

I cup water

I tsp. low-sodium teriyaki sauce

1. Cut beef into ¼-inch-wide strips.

2. In a good-sized skillet, stir-fry beef in 2 tsp. olive oil just until no longer pink, about 2 minutes.

3. Add onion and other vegetables. Stir-fry until tender-crisp, about 5–7 minutes.

4. To cook rice, place rice and water in a saucepan. Cover, and bring to a boil. Adjust heat so that mixture simmers, covered. Cook rice until tender, about 20–25 minutes.

5. Just before serving over rice, add teriyaki sauce to beef and vegetables.

Fabulous Fajitas

Phyllis Good, Lancaster, PA

Makes 4 servings

Prep. Time: 15 minutes ⚘ *Cooking Time: 3½ hours* ⚘ *Ideal slow-cooker size: 4-qt.*

1–1½ lb. flank steak, cut across grain in ½-inch-thick strips

2 Tbsp. lemon juice

1 clove garlic, minced

1½ tsp. cumin

½ tsp. red pepper flakes

1 tsp. seasoning salt

2 Tbsp. Worcestershire sauce

1 tsp. chili powder

1 green bell pepper, cut in strips

1 yellow onion, sliced

6–8 warmed tortillas, for serving

Favorite toppings:

Sour cream

Chopped fresh cilantro

Salsa

Shredded cheese

1. Grease interior of slow-cooker crock.

2. Place beef strips in crock.

3. Stir in lemon juice, garlic, cumin, red pepper flakes, seasoning salt, Worcestershire sauce, and chili powder.

4. Cook on Low 2½ hours, or until beef is nearly tender.

5. Stir in pepper and onion.

6. Cover. Cook for another hour on Low or until vegetables are as tender as you like them.

7. Spoon mixture into warm tortillas. Top with favorite toppings.

Easy Chicken Fajitas

Jessica Hontz, Coatesville, PA

Makes 4–6 servings

Prep. Time: 20 minutes 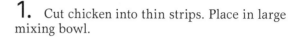 *Marinating Time: 4–8 hours, or overnight* *Cooking Time: 10 minutes*

1 lb. boneless, skinless chicken breasts
1 pkg. dry Italian salad dressing mix
8-oz. bottle Italian salad dressing
1 cup salsa
1 green pepper, sliced
½ medium-sized onion, sliced
10 (10-inch) flour tortillas

Optional toppings:
Shredded Monterey Jack cheese
Shredded lettuce
Sour cream
Chopped tomatoes
Salsa
Hot pepper sauce

1. Cut chicken into thin strips. Place in large mixing bowl.

2. Add dry salad dressing mix and salad dressing. Mix well. Cover and marinate 4–8 hours in the fridge.

3. In a large skillet, combine drained chicken strips, salsa, and pepper and onion slices. Stir-fry until chicken is cooked and peppers and onion are soft.

4. Place chicken mix in tortillas with your choice of toppings.

Variation:

The cooked chicken can also be used on salads.

Herby French Dip Sandwiches

SLOW COOKER

Sara Wichert, Hillsboro, KS

Makes 6–8 servings

Prep. Time: 5 minutes   Cooking Time: 5–6 hours   Ideal slow-cooker size: 4-qt.

3-lb. chuck roast

2 cups water

½ cup gluten-free, low-sodium soy sauce or liquid aminos

1 tsp. garlic powder

1 bay leaf

3–4 whole peppercorns

1 tsp. dried rosemary, *optional*

1 tsp. dried thyme, *optional*

1. Place roast in the slow cooker.

2. Combine remaining ingredients in a mixing bowl. Pour over meat.

3. Cover and cook on High 5–6 hours, or until meat is tender but not dry.

4. Remove bay leaf and discard. Remove meat from broth and shred with fork. Stir back into sauce.

5. Remove meat from the cooker by large forkfuls.

Serving suggestion:

Serve on French rolls.

Beef and Pepperoncini Hoagies

SLOW COOKER

Donna Treloar, Muncie, IN

Makes 10 servings (varies with roast size)

Prep. Time: 15 minutes 🌿 Cooking Time: 8–10 hours 🌿 Ideal slow-cooker size: 5- or 6-qt.

3–5-lb. boneless chuck roast (inexpensive cuts work fine)

Salt and pepper to taste

I clove garlic, minced, or I tsp. garlic powder

16-oz. jar of pepperoncini peppers, mild or medium, depending on your preference

Hoagie rolls or buns of your choice

20 slices provolone cheese

Variations:

This is excellent as is, but I frequently add chopped onions to Step 7 . . . just because we love onions. You can also add a package of dry Italian dressing mix and a cup or two of beef broth to Steps 7 and 8.   Or you can add a package of Lipton Onion Soup Mix along with beef and chicken broth. It's hard to hurt this recipe!

Serving suggestion:

Goes well with sweet potato fries.

1. Grease interior of slow-cooker crock.

2. Trim roast of fat.

3. Salt and pepper to taste, holding over crock.

4. If using garlic powder, sprinkle on all sides of beef over crock. Place beef in crock.

5. If using minced garlic, scatter over beef in crock.

6. If the pepperoncini peppers are whole and have stems, remove peppers from jar and cut up. Reserve liquid.

7. Scatter cut-up peppers over meat.

8. Pour liquid from peppers down alongside of crock interior so you don't wash off the seasonings.

9. Cover. Cook on low 7½–9½ hours, or until beef registers 160°F on an instant-read meat thermometer when stuck in center of roast.

10. Lift roast into a big bowl and shred with two forks.

11. Stir shredded meat back into juices in crock.

12. Cover. Cook another 30 minutes on Low.

13. When ready to serve, use a slotted spoon to drain meat well.

14. Spoon well-drained meat onto a hoagie roll and top each sandwich with 2 slices cheese.

Sloppy Joes

Hope Comerford, Clinton Township, MI

Makes 15–18 servings

Prep. Time: 25 minutes ♣ *Cooking Time: 6–7 hours* ♣ *Ideal slow-cooker size: 6-qt.*

1½ lb. extra-lean ground beef

16 oz. ground turkey sausage

½ large red onion, chopped

½ green bell pepper, chopped

8-oz. can low-sodium tomato sauce

½ cup water

½ cup ketchup

¼ cup tightly packed brown sugar

2 Tbsp. apple cider vinegar

2 Tbsp. yellow mustard

1 Tbsp. gluten-free Worcestershire sauce

1 Tbsp. chili powder

1 tsp. garlic powder

1 tsp. onion powder

¼ tsp. salt

¼ tsp. pepper

1. Brown the ground beef and sausage in a pan. Drain all grease.

2. While the beef and sausage are cooking, mix the remaining ingredients in the crock.

3. Add the cooked beef and sausage to the crock and mix.

4. Cover and cook on Low for 6–7 hours.

Serving suggestion:

Serve on hamburger buns.

BBQ Chicken Sandwiches

Sarah Herr, Goshen, IN

Makes 8 servings

Prep. Time: 15 minutes   ⚬   *Cooking Time: 4 hours*   ⚬   *Ideal slow-cooker size: 5-qt.*

3 lb. boneless, skinless chicken thighs

1 onion, chopped

½ cup brown sugar

½ cup apple cider vinegar

½ cup ketchup

1 tsp. dry mustard

1 tsp. cumin

1 Tbsp. chili powder

½ tsp. black pepper

8 hamburger buns

1. Grease interior of slow-cooker crock.

2. Place chicken into crock. If you need to make a second layer, stagger the pieces so they don't directly overlap each other.

3. Mix other ingredients together well in a bowl.

4. Spoon over thighs. Make sure the ones on the bottom layer get covered, too.

5. Cover. Cook on Low 4 hours, or until instant read meat thermometer registers 160°F when stuck in center of thighs.

6. Lift cooked chicken out of crock and shred with two forks.

7. Stir shredded meat back into sauce in crock.

8. Serve on hamburger buns.

Walking Tacos

SLOW COOKER

Hope Comerford, Clinton Township, MI

Makes 10–16 servings

Prep. Time: 10 minutes   &   Cooking Time: 6–7 hours   &   Ideal slow-cooker size: 2–3 qt.

2 lb. ground beef

2 tsp. garlic powder

2 tsp. onion powder

1 Tbsp. cumin

2 Tbsp. chili powder

1 tsp. salt

½ tsp. oregano

½ tsp. red pepper flakes

1 small onion, minced

1 clove garlic, minced

10–16 individual sized bags of Doritos

Suggested toppings:

Diced tomatoes

Shredded cheese

Diced cucumbers

Chopped onion

Shredded lettuce

Sour cream

Salsa

1. Crumble the ground beef into the crock.

2. In a bowl, mix all the spices, onion, and garlic. Pour this over beef then stir it up.

3. Cover and cook for 6–7 hours, breaking it up occasionally with a spoon.

4. Remove some of the grease if you wish.

5. To serve, open the bag of Doritos, crumble the chips in the bag with your hand, add some of the ground beef to the bag, then any additional toppings you desire. Serve each bag with a fork.

Carnitas Tacos

MarJanita Martin, Batesburg, SC

Makes 8–10 servings

Prep. Time: 30 minutes   ♣   Cooking Time: 6 hours   ♣   Ideal slow-cooker size: 6–7 qt.

2 cups uncooked rice

4–5 lb. boneless pork loin

24 (6-inch) flour and corn tortillas, for serving

2 cups shredded cheese, for serving

8 oz. sour cream, for serving

Rub:

3 Tbsp. brown sugar

1 Tbsp. salt

1 Tbsp. pepper

1 tsp. paprika

1 tsp. dried oregano

½ tsp. red pepper

1 Tbsp. garlic powder

Pineapple Salsa:

20-oz. can pineapple tidbits, drained

½ jalapeño pepper, minced

½ red onion, diced

¼ cup chopped cilantro

Juice of ½ lime

2 Tbsp. lemon juice

1. Cook rice as directed by package.

2. Mix together rub ingredients and rub into the pork loin.

3. Mix together ingredients for the pineapple salsa, then place in the refrigerator while the loin cooks.

4. Put pork loin into a greased slow cooker.

5. Cover and cook on Low for 6 hours.

6. Shred the pork.

7. Serve into tortilla shells.

8. Top with rice, cheese, salsa, and sour cream.

Tip:

Good for weekdays and weekends!

Oven Enchiladas

Melanie Thrower, McPherson, KS

Makes 8 servings

Prep. Time: 15 minutes ☙ *Cooking/Baking Time: 30 minutes*

1 lb. ground beef

2 medium-sized yellow onions, chopped

16 corn tortillas

2 cups shredded Mexican cheese

2 (16-oz.) cans green chili or red enchilada sauce

1. In a skillet, brown ground beef. Drain off drippings.

2. Heat tortillas in nonstick pan to make them flexible.

3. Fill each tortilla with browned beef, topped with onion. Roll up, tuck in sides, and continue rolling. Place side-by-side on a baking sheet with sides.

4. Sprinkle cheese over top of filled enchiladas. Pour sauce over top.

5. Cover with aluminum foil. Bake at 375°F for 30 minutes.

Serving suggestion:

Serve with dishes of sour cream, salsa, and guacamole as optional toppings.

Slow Cooker Burritos

Hope Comerford, Clinton Township, MI

Makes 8 servings

Prep. Time: 10 minutes & Cooking Time: 5 hours & Ideal slow-cooker size: 3-qt.

1½ lb. boneless skinless chicken breasts

15-oz. can pinto beans, rinsed and drained

2 cups salsa

1 cup chicken stock

1 small onion, chopped

4-oz. can diced green chilies

1 cup frozen corn

2 Tbsp. chili powder

1 tsp. cumin

1½ tsp. salt

½ cup brown rice

8 round flour tortillas

1. Place the chicken in the crock.

2. In a bowl, mix the pinto beans, salsa, chicken stock, onion, green chilies, corn, chili powder, cumin, and salt. Pour this over the chicken.

3. Cover and cook on Low for 3 hours. Stir in the rice.

4. Cover again and cook on Low for an additional 2 hours.

5. Remove and shred the chicken between two forks. Stir it back through the contents of the crock.

6. Fill each tortilla with the burrito filling and wrap them up.

Mexican Chicken Stack

Diann Dunham, State College, PA

Makes 6 servings

Prep. Time: 30 minutes ⚓ *Baking Time: 25 minutes*

1½–2 cups shredded rotisserie chicken meat

1 green bell pepper, chopped

¼ cup chopped onion

1 tsp. ground cumin

1½ cups chunky salsa

3-oz. pkg. cream cheese, softened

11-oz. can Southwestern corn (mixture of corn, peppers, black beans), drained

3 (10–12-inch) flour tortillas, *divided*

1 cup shredded Mexican cheese, *divided*

Serving suggestions:

1. Pass extra salsa so diners can add to their individual servings if they wish.

2. Sprinkle chopped cilantro on top before serving.

1. Warm chicken, bell pepper, and onion in a nonstick skillet over low heat.

2. Stir in cumin and salsa.

3. Cook 2 minutes.

4. Add cream cheese and cook, stirring, 2 minutes until melted.

5. Stir in corn.

6. Spray an 8 × 8-inch baking dish with nonstick cooking spray.

7. Put 1 tortilla in dish. Stack in ⅓ of chicken mixture, and then 1 tortilla, ½ of remaining chicken mixture, and ¼ cup shredded cheese.

8. Add last tortilla, and remaining chicken mixture.

9. Cover with foil. Bake 20 minutes.

10. Uncover. Add remaining cheese.

11. Bake uncovered until cheese melts, about 5 minutes. Allow stack to rest 10 minutes before serving. Cut in wedges or squares.

Shepherd's Pie

Judi Manos, West Islip, NY

Makes 6 servings

Prep. Time: 15 minutes ⚘ *Cooking/Baking Time: 50 minutes*

1¼ lb. red potatoes, unpeeled and cut in chunks

3 cloves garlic

1 lb. 95%-lean ground beef

2 Tbsp. flour

4 cups fresh vegetables of your choice (for example, carrots, corn, green beans, peas)

¾ cup beef broth, canned, or boxed, or your own homemade

2 Tbsp. ketchup

¾ cup fat-free sour cream

½ cup shredded reduced-fat sharp cheddar cheese, *divided*

Variation:

If you don't have access to fresh vegetables, use leftovers from your fridge or frozen ones.

1. In saucepan, cook potatoes and garlic in 1½ inches boiling water for 20 minutes, or until potatoes are tender.

2. Meanwhile, brown beef in large nonstick skillet.

3. Stir in flour. Cook 1 minute.

4. Stir in vegetables, broth, and ketchup. Cover. Cook 10 minutes, stirring frequently.

5. Drain cooked potatoes and garlic. Return to their pan.

6. Stir in sour cream. Mash until potatoes are smooth and mixture is well blended.

7. Stir ¼ cup cheddar cheese into mashed potatoes.

8. Spoon meat mixture into well-greased 8 × 8-inch baking dish.

9. Cover with mashed potatoes.

10. Bake at 375°F for 18 minutes.

11. Top with remaining cheddar cheese. Bake 2 minutes more, or until cheese is melted.

Stuffed Green Peppers

SLOW COOKER

Lois Stoltzfus, Honey Brook, PA

Makes 6 servings

Prep. Time: 20 minutes ♣ *Cooking Time: 3–8 hours* ♣ *Ideal slow-cooker size: 5- to 6-qt.*

6 large green peppers

1 lb. extra-lean ground beef, browned

2 Tbsp. minced onion

1 tsp. salt

⅛ tsp. garlic powder

2 cups cooked rice

15-oz. can low-sodium tomato sauce

¾ cup shredded low-fat mozzarella cheese

1. Cut peppers in half and remove seeds.

2. Combine all ingredients except peppers and cheese.

3. Stuff peppers with ground beef mixture. Place in slow cooker.

4. Cover. Cook on Low 6–8 hours, or on High 3–4 hours. Sprinkle with cheese during last 30 minutes.

Upside-Down Pizza

Julia Rohrer, Aaronsburg, PA
Janet L. Roggie, Lowville, NY

Makes 10 servings, 2½ × 4½-inch rectangle

Prep. Time: 20–30 minutes ⚓ Baking Time: 25–30 minutes

14 oz. 95%-lean ground beef

1 chopped onion

1 medium red, or green, bell pepper, chopped

1 tsp. dried basil

1 tsp. dried oregano

2 cups pizza, or spaghetti, sauce

¼ lb. fresh mushrooms, chopped, or 4-oz. can chopped mushrooms, drained

1 cup grated part-skim mozzarella cheese

Batter:

¾ cup egg substitute

1½ cups fat-free milk

1½ Tbsp. oil

½ tsp. salt

1 tsp. baking soda

1¾ cups flour

Sprinkle of dried oregano

Sprinkle of grated Parmesan cheese

1. Brown meat with onion and pepper in large nonstick skillet.

2. Stir in seasonings, sauce, and mushrooms. Simmer 5–8 minutes.

3. Place in well-greased 9 × 13-inch baking pan.

4. Cover with grated cheese.

5. Prepare batter by beating egg substitute, milk, and oil together in good-sized mixing bowl.

6. Add salt, baking soda, and flour. Stir just until mixed.

7. Pour over cheese-meat mixture. Do not stir.

8. Sprinkle with oregano and Parmesan cheese.

9. Bake at 400°F for 25–30 minutes or until toothpick inserted in center of dough comes out clean.

Grandma's Best Meatloaf

Nanci Keatley, Salem, OR

Makes 10 servings, 1 slice per serving

Prep. Time: 15–25 minutes & *Baking Time: 1 hour 5 minutes* & *Standing Time: 10 minutes*

2 lb. 90%-lean ground beef

2 Tbsp. chopped fresh Italian parsley

I tsp. dried oregano

I small onion, chopped fine

4 cloves garlic, minced

¼ cup plus 2 Tbsp. Romano cheese, *optional*

½ cup dried bread crumbs

½ cup ketchup

½ cup egg substitute

I tsp. black pepper

I tsp. kosher salt

1. In a large mixing bowl, mix together ground beef, parsley, oregano, onion, garlic, cheese (optional), bread crumbs, ketchup, egg substitute, pepper, and salt.

2. Roll mixture into a large ball.

3. Place in well-greased 9 × 13-inch baking dish or roaster, flattening slightly.

4. Bake at 375°F for 1 hour. Keep in oven 5 more minutes with oven off and door closed.

5. Remove meatloaf from oven. Let stand 10 minutes before slicing to allow meatloaf to gather its juices and firm up.

Taco Meatloaf

Tammy Smith, Dorchester, WI

Makes 8 servings

Prep. Time: 20 minutes ⚬ *Cooking Time: 4 hours* ⚬ *Ideal slow-cooker size: oval 5- or 6-qt.*

3 eggs, lightly beaten
½ cup crushed tomatoes
¾ cup crushed tortilla chips
1 medium onion, finely chopped
2 cloves garlic, minced
3 tsp. taco seasoning
2 tsp. chili powder
1 lb. ground beef
1 lb. ground pork
½ tsp. salt
¾ tsp. black pepper

1. Grease interior of slow-cooker crock.

2. Make a tinfoil sling for your slow cooker so you can lift the cooked meatloaf out easily. Begin by folding a strip of foil accordion-fashion so that it's about 1½–2 inches wide, and long enough to fit from the top edge of the crock, down inside and up the other side, plus a 2-inch overhang on each side of the cooker. Make a second strip exactly like the first.

3. Place one strip in crock, running from end to end. Place second strip in crock, running from side to side. The strips should form a cross in bottom of the crock.

4. In a large bowl, combine all ingredients well.

5. Shape into a loaf. Place into crock so that the center of loaf sits where the two strips of foil cross.

6. Cover. Cook for 4 hours on Low.

7. Using the foil handles, lift loaf onto platter. Cover to keep warm. Let stand for 10–15 minutes before slicing.

Glazed Barbecue Turkey Meatloaf

Hope Comerford, Clinton Township, MI

Makes 6–8 servings

Prep. Time: 15–20 minutes ⚜ *Cooking Time: 4–5 hours* ⚜ *Ideal slow-cooker size: 5-qt. oval*

2 lb. ground turkey

1 large egg

1 ¼ cups gluten-free or regular panko bread crumbs

1 Tbsp. garlic powder

1 Tbsp. onion powder

3 tsp. dried minced onion

1 tsp. Italian seasoning

6 dashes Worcestershire sauce

¼ cup barbecue sauce

Glaze:

3 Tbsp. brown sugar

¼ cup barbecue sauce

1 tsp. dry mustard

1. Spray crock with nonstick spray.

2. Make a tinfoil sling for your slow cooker so you can lift the cooked meatloaf out easily. Begin by folding a strip of foil accordion-fashion so that it's about 1½–2 inches wide, and long enough to fit from the top edge of the crock, down inside and up the other side, plus a 2-inch overhang on each side of the cooker. Make a second strip exactly like the first.

3. Place the first strip in the crock, running from end to end. Place the second strip in the crock, running from side to side. The 2 strips should form a cross in the bottom of the crock.

4. In a bowl, mix all of the meatloaf ingredients, then shape it into a loaf. Place it in the crock, centering it where the foil handles cross.

5. Cover and cook on Low 4–5 hours.

6. Remove the meatloaf from the crock using the handles and place on a baking sheet.

7. Mix the glaze ingredients together. Spoon this over the top of the meatloaf.

8. Place the meatloaf in the oven under the broiler for 2–4 minutes, so that the glaze thickens and browns, but be careful not to let it burn.

9. Let it stand for 10 minutes, then slice and serve.

Country Gal's Chicken Pot Pie

MarJanita Martin, Batesburg, SC

Makes 4–6 servings

Prep. Time: 30 minutes & Baking Time: 45 minutes

2 refrigerated pie crusts

2 Tbsp. butter

12½-oz. canned chicken, drained

1 tsp. seasoned salt

½ tsp. pepper

2½ cups frozen mixed vegetables

1 cup shredded cheese

1 egg, beaten

1 Tbsp. water

Sauce:

3 Tbsp. butter

1 medium onion, sliced

⅓ cup flour

½ tsp. salt

½ tsp. pepper

1 Tbsp. Italian seasoning

1 sprig rosemary, chopped

2 basil leaves, chopped

1¾ cups chicken stock

⅔ cups half-and-half

1. Put one crust in the pie dish. Prick the bottom crust with a fork.

2. Melt the 2 Tbsp. of butter in a large saucepan.

3. Add chicken, seasoned salt, and pepper.

4. Add in veggies and cook until almost tender.

5. Remove from saucepan and set aside.

6. Make the sauce: Use the saucepan and melt the 3 Tbsp. of butter.

7. Add the onion and cook until translucent.

8. Whisk in flour, salt, pepper, Italian seasoning, rosemary, and basil.

9. Pour in chicken stock and half-and-half, stirring constantly. Simmer until thickened.

10. Add veggies and chicken into the sauce. Gently stir. Pour this mixture into pie dish.

11. Add the shredded cheese over top, then place other crust over top.

12. Seal and crimp edges, while cutting away any excess dough. Slit the crust.

13. Whisk together egg and water. Brush over the top of the pie.

14. Bake at 350°F for 45 minutes.

15. Remove and let stand 10 minutes before serving.

Crustless Chicken Pot Pie

Hope Comerford, Clinton Township, MI

Makes 6 servings

Prep. Time: 15 minutes   Cook Time: 30 minutes

1 lb. boneless, skinless chicken breasts

3 Yukon Gold potatoes, peeled and chopped into ½-inch cubes

1 cup chopped onion

2 carrots, chopped

¾ cup frozen peas

¾ cup frozen corn

½ cup chopped celery

10½-oz. can condensed cream of chicken soup

1 cup milk

1 cup chicken broth

1 tsp. salt

1 tsp. garlic powder

1 tsp. onion powder

2 Tbsp. cornstarch

2 Tbsp. cold water

16.3-oz. can flaky biscuits

1. Place all ingredients, except for the cornstarch, water, and biscuits, into the inner pot of the Instant Pot.

2. Secure the lid and set the vent to sealing. Manually set the cook time for 25 minutes on high pressure.

3. While the Instant Pot is cooking, bake the canned biscuits according to the directions on the can.

4. When the cook time is over, manually release the pressure.

5. When the pin drops, remove the lid. Remove the chicken to a bowl. Press Cancel then press Sauté.

6. Mix together the cornstarch and water. Stir this into the contents of the Instant Pot and cook until thickened, about 5 minutes. Meanwhile, shred the chicken, then add it back in with the contents of the inner pot.

7. Serve with the freshly baked flaky biscuits.

Chicken and Biscuits

Hope Comerford, Clinton Township, MI

Makes 4–6 servings

Prep. Time: 5 minutes ❧ *Cooking Time: 6 hours* ❧ *Ideal slow-cooker size: 3-qt.*

2 lb. boneless skinless chicken breasts

10½-oz. can condensed cream of chicken soup

10½-oz. can condensed cream of potato soup

¾ cup milk

½ tsp. salt

⅛ tsp. pepper

2 tsp. garlic powder

2 tsp. onion powder

1 cup frozen mixed vegetables

6 refrigerator biscuits, cooked according to the package directions

1. Place the boneless skinless chicken in the crock.

2. In a bowl, mix the cream of chicken soup, cream of potato soup, milk, salt, pepper, garlic powder, onion powder, and frozen mixed vegetables. Pour this over the chicken.

3. Cover and cook on Low for 6 hours.

4. Shred the chicken between two forks and stir back through the contents of the crock.

5. Serve the chicken mixture over the biscuits.

Instant Pot Chicken and Dumplings

Bonnie Miller, Louisville, OH

Makes 4 servings

Prep. Time: 10 minutes   *Cook Time: 3 minutes*

1 Tbsp. olive oil

1 small onion, chopped

2 celery ribs, cut into 1-inch pieces

6 small carrots, cut into 1-inch chunks

2 cups chicken broth

2 lb. boneless, skinless chicken breast halves, cut into 1-inch pieces

2 chicken bouillon cubes

1 tsp. salt

1 tsp. pepper

1 tsp. poultry seasoning

Biscuits:

2 cups buttermilk biscuit mix

½ cup plus 1 Tbsp. milk

1 tsp. parsley

1. Set the Instant Pot to the Sauté function and heat the olive oil.

2. Add the onion, celery, and carrots to the hot oil and sauté for 3 to 5 minutes.

3. Pour in the broth and scrape the bottom of the inner pot with a wooden spoon or spatula to deglaze. Press Cancel.

4. Add the chicken, bouillon, salt, pepper, and poultry seasoning.

5. Combine the biscuit ingredients in a bowl until just moistened. Drop 2-tablespoon mounds over the contents of the inner pot, as evenly spaced out as possible.

6. Secure the lid and set the vent to sealing. Manually set the cook time for 3 minutes.

7. When the cook time is over, manually release the pressure.

Pizzas

Crazy Crust Pizza

Pamela Metzler, Gilman, WI

Makes 8 servings

Prep. Time: 20 minutes ❧ *Baking Time: 20 minutes* ❧ *Standing Time: 5 minutes*

2 cups flour

4 eggs

2½ tsp. salt, *divided*

1½ cups milk

1 lb. ground beef, or sausage

½–1 cup chopped onion, according to your taste preference

2 tsp. dried oregano

Pepper to taste

26-oz. can tomato sauce

½–1 cup shredded mozzarella cheese

½–1 cup shredded cheddar cheese

1. In a mixing bowl, mix the flour, eggs, 2 tsp. salt, and milk until smooth. Pour into a greased and floured jelly-roll pan.

2. In a large skillet, brown ground beef and onion. Season with oregano, ½ tsp. salt, and pepper. Stir in tomato sauce. Pour over crust.

3. Sprinkle cheeses evenly over top.

4. Bake at 475°F for 20 minutes. Let stand 5 minutes before cutting.

Chicken Fajita Pizza

Ann Henderson, Cincinnati, OH

Makes 6–8 servings

Prep. Time: 20–30 minutes ❧ Baking Time: 15–20 minutes

1 Tbsp. oil

1 small boneless, skinless chicken breast, about ¾ lb., cut into 2 × ½-inch strips

1 clove garlic, pressed, or ½ tsp. garlic powder

1–2 tsp. chili powder, according to your taste preference

½ tsp. salt

1 cup thinly sliced onion

1 cup combination of green, red, and orange pepper slices

10-oz. pkg. refrigerated pizza crust

Cornmeal

½ cup salsa or picante sauce

2 cups shredded Monterey Jack cheese

1. Heat oil in skillet. Add chicken strips and stir-fry just until lightly browned.

2. Stir in garlic, chili powder, and salt. Add onion and peppers and cook for 1 minute until tender-crisp.

3. Unroll dough and roll onto cornmeal-covered pizza stone. Par-bake dough at 425°F for 8–10 minutes.

4. Spoon chicken and vegetable mixture onto crust. Cover with salsa and cheese.

5. Bake at 425°F for about 5 more minutes, or until crust is browning.

Barbecue Chicken Pizza

Hope Comerford, Clinton Township, MI

Makes 6 servings

Prep. Time: 10 minutes & *Cooking/Baking Time: 13–15 minutes*

14 oz. premade or homemade pizza dough

½ cup sliced red onion pieces

1 Tbsp. olive oil

1½ cups diced rotisserie chicken meat

1½ cups of your favorite barbecue sauce, *divided*

3 cups mozzarella cheese

⅓ cup chopped fresh cilantro

1. Spread pizza dough on a pizza pan and bake for 5 minutes at whatever temperature the packaging suggests.

2. While the pizza dough is cooking, sauté the red onion pieces in the olive oil until they are translucent. Set aside.

3. When the pizza crust has finished its 5 minutes, remove it.

4. Spread ½ cup of the barbecue sauce over the pizza crust.

5. Toss the rotisserie chicken meat with the remaining barbecue sauce and arrange it on the pizza crust.

6. Arrange the sautéed red onion pieces on the pizza crust.

7. Sprinkle the mozzarella cheese evenly over the toppings on the pizza.

8. Bake the pizza for 8–10 minutes, or until the cheese is melted and crust is golden brown.

9. When you remove the pizza, sprinkle it with the cilantro.

10. Serve and enjoy!

Mexican Pizza

Erma Martin, East Earl, PA
Ruth Ann Bender, Cochranville, PA

Makes 12–16 servings

Preparation Time: 30 minutes   Baking Time: 8–10 minutes

2 (8-oz.) tubes refrigerated crescent rolls

8-oz. pkg. cream cheese, softened

1 cup sour cream

1 lb. ground beef

1 envelope dry taco seasoning mix

2¼-oz. can sliced ripe olives, drained

1 medium tomato, chopped

¾ cup shredded cheddar cheese

¾ cup shredded mozzarella cheese

1 cup shredded lettuce

1. Flatten crescent rolls onto an ungreased 10 × 15-inch baking pan. Seal the seams.

2. Bake at 375°F for 8–10 minutes. Cool.

3. Meanwhile, combine cream cheese and sour cream. Spread on cooled crust.

4. Brown beef in a skillet. Drain off drippings. Stir in taco seasoning. Add water according to seasoning package directions. Simmer for 5 minutes.

5. Spread meat over cream cheese layer.

6. Layer olives, tomato, cheeses, and lettuce over top.

7. Cut into serving size pieces. Refrigerate or serve immediately.

Variations:

1. Add ¼ cup chopped onion and ½ cup chopped green pepper to the toppings in Step 6.

2. Replace taco seasoning and water in Step 4 with 1 minced garlic clove, ¼ cup chopped green chilies, ¼ tsp. dried oregano, ½ tsp. salt, and a scant ½ tsp. cumin powder. Simmer for 5 minutes; then proceed with rest of the recipe.

—Bonita Ensenberger, Albuquerque, NM

Pastas

Flavorful Beef Stroganoff

Susan Guarneri, Three Lakes, WI

Makes 6 servings

Prep. Time: 25 minutes ⚬ *Cooking Time: 1 hour 20 minutes*

2 lb. boneless chuck

¼ cup flour

1 tsp. salt

2 Tbsp. butter

1 medium-sized onion, chopped

1 clove garlic, crushed

10¾-oz. can cream of mushroom soup

½ tsp. cinnamon

¼ tsp. allspice

1 cup water

4-oz. can sliced mushrooms, undrained

1 pt. sour cream

Egg noodles

1. Cut chuck in strips ½-inch thick.

2. Mix flour and salt. Dredge meat in flour/salt mixture.

3. Melt butter in large skillet. Brown flour-coated meat in butter over high heat. Stir often so that meat browns on all sides.

4. When meat is browned, turn down heat and add onion, garlic, soup, cinnamon, allspice, and water.

5. Cover and simmer 1 hour.

6. Reduce heat and stir in mushrooms and sour cream. Do not allow to boil, but simmer, covered, until heated through. Serve over egg noodles.

Slow-Cooker Beef Stroganoff

Becky Fixel, Grosse Pointe Farms, MI

Makes 6–8 servings

Prep. Time: 10 minutes   *Cooking Time: 6 hours*   *Ideal slow-cooker size: 5-qt.*

1 cup nonfat plain Greek yogurt
8 oz. reduced-fat cream cheese
¼ cup condensed mushroom soup mix
1 medium onion, minced
½ stick (4 Tbsp.) butter
1 lb. stew beef
⅛ tsp. paprika
8–10 oz. mushrooms, sliced
½ cup fat-free milk
1 tsp. salt
1 tsp. pepper

1. Mix yogurt, cream cheese, and mushroom soup mix in medium bowl.

2. Add all ingredients to your crock and mix well.

3. Cover and cook on Low for 6 hours. You may stir occasionally.

Lasagna

Colleen Heatwole, Burton, MI

Makes 8–12 servings

Prep. Time: 45 minutes ❧ Baking Time: 30 minutes

1 lb. ground beef
1 clove garlic, minced
1 scant Tbsp. basil
¾ tsp. salt
28- to 32-oz. can stewed tomatoes, or 28-oz. jar pasta sauce
6-oz. can tomato paste
½ tsp. oregano
10 oz. lasagna noodles, *divided*
3 cups cottage cheese
½ cup grated Parmesan cheese
1 lb. mozzarella cheese, grated
2 Tbsp. parsley flakes
2 eggs, beaten
½ tsp. pepper

1. Brown beef slowly in stockpot. Stir frequently to break up clumps. Pour off drippings.

2. Stir in garlic, basil, salt, tomatoes or pasta sauce, tomato paste, and oregano. Mix well.

3. Simmer, uncovered, 30 minutes.

4. Meanwhile, cook pasta al dente, according to package directions. Drain well.

5. In large bowl, combine cottage cheese, Parmesan cheese, mozzarella cheese, parsley flakes, beaten eggs, and pepper.

6. Place half the noodles in greased 9 × 13-inch baking dish.

7. Cover with half the meat sauce.

8. Top with half the cheese mixture.

9. Repeat layers, ending with cheese mixture.

10. Bake at 375°F for 30 minutes, or until bubbly and heated through.

Tip:

You can assemble this lasagna ahead of time through Step 9. Cover and refrigerate. When ready to bake, allow 15 minutes longer in oven, or bake at 200°F for 2 hours if baking during church for a noon potluck. Cover during baking if baking 2 hours.

Variation:

Instead of ground beef, use ½ lb. bulk hot Italian sausage. Brown it as instructed for ground beef and drain off drippings.

—Monica Leaman Kehr, Portland, MI

Lasagna the Instant Pot Way

Hope Comerford, Clinton Township, MI

Makes 8 servings

Prep. Time: 15 minutes & *Cook Time: 15 minutes*

1 Tbsp. olive oil

1 lb. extra-lean ground beef or ground turkey

½ cup chopped onion

½ tsp. salt

⅛ tsp. pepper

2 cups water

12 lasagna noodles

8 oz. cottage cheese

1 egg

1 tsp. Italian seasoning

4 cups spinach, chopped or torn

1 cup sliced mushrooms

28 oz. marinara sauce

1 cup mozzarella cheese

1. Set the Instant Pot to the Sauté function and heat the olive oil. Brown the beef and onion with the salt and pepper. This will take about 5 minutes. Because you're using extra-lean ground beef, there should not be much grease, but if so, you'll need to drain it before continuing. Remove half of the ground beef and set aside. Press Cancel.

2. Pour in the water.

3. Break 4 noodles in half and arrange them on top of the beef and water.

4. Mix together the cottage cheese, egg, and Italian seasoning until the mixture is smooth. Smooth half of this mixture over the lasagna noodles.

5. Layer half of the spinach and half of the mushrooms on top.

6. Break 4 more noodles in half and lay them on top of what you just did. Spread out the remaining cottage cheese mixture.

7. Layer on the remaining spinach and mushrooms, then pour half of the marinara sauce over the top.

8. Finish with breaking the remaining 4 noodles in half and laying them on top of the previous layer. Spread the remaining marinara sauce on top.

9. Secure the lid and set the vent to sealing. Manually set the cook time for 7 minutes on high pressure.

10. When the cook time is over, let the pressure release naturally for 10 minutes, then manually release the remaining pressure.

11. When the pin drops, remove the lid and sprinkle the mozzarella cheese on top. Re-cover for 5 minutes.

12. When the 5 minutes is up, remove the lid. You can let this sit for a while to thicken up on "Keep Warm."

Convenient Slow-Cooker Lasagna

Rachel Yoder, Middlebury, IN

Makes 6–8 servings

Prep. Time: 30–45 minutes   Cooking Time: 4 hours   Ideal slow-cooker size: 6-qt.

1 lb. extra-lean ground beef

29-oz. can tomato sauce

8-oz. pkg. lasagna noodles, uncooked, *divided*

4 cups shredded low-fat mozzarella cheese

1 ½ cups low-fat cottage cheese

1. Spray the interior of the cooker with nonstick spray.

2. Brown the ground beef in a large nonstick skillet. Drain off drippings.

3. Stir in tomato sauce. Mix well.

4. Spread one-fourth of the meat sauce on the bottom of the slow cooker.

5. Arrange ⅓ of the uncooked noodles over the sauce. If you wish, break them up so they fit better.

6. Combine the cheeses in a bowl. Spoon ⅓ of the cheeses over the noodles.

7. Repeat these layers twice.

8. Top with remaining meat sauce.

9. Cover and cook on Low 4 hours.

Fresh Veggie Lasagna

Deanne Gingrich, Lancaster, PA

Makes 4–6 servings

Prep. Time: 30 minutes ⚜ *Cooking Time: 4 hours* ⚜ *Ideal slow-cooker size: 4- or 5-qt.*

1½ cups shredded mozzarella cheese

½ cup ricotta cheese

⅓ cup grated Parmesan cheese

1 egg, lightly beaten

1 tsp. dried oregano

¼ tsp. garlic powder

3 cups marinara sauce, *divided*, plus more for serving

1 medium zucchini, diced, *divided*

4 uncooked lasagna noodles

4 cups fresh baby spinach, *divided*

1 cup fresh mushrooms, sliced, *divided*

1. Grease interior of slow-cooker crock.

2. In a bowl, mix the mozzarella, ricotta, and Parmesan cheeses, egg, oregano, and garlic powder. Set aside.

3. Spread ½ cup marinara sauce in crock.

4. Sprinkle with half the zucchini.

5. Spoon ⅓ of cheese mixture over zucchini.

6. Break 2 noodles into large pieces to cover cheese layer.

7. Spread ½ cup marinara over noodles.

8. Top with half the spinach and then half the mushrooms.

9. Repeat layers, ending with cheese mixture, and then sauce. Press layers down firmly.

10. Cover. Cook on Low 4 hours, or until vegetables are as tender as you like them and noodles are fully cooked.

11. Let stand 15 minutes so lasagna can firm up before serving.

Household-Size Ziti Bake

Joy Reiff, Mount Joy, PA

Makes 6–8 servings

Prep. Time: 30 minutes ☂ *Baking Time: 45–60 minutes*

1 lb. ziti, or rigatoni
1¼ lb. ground beef
1 lb. ricotta, or cottage, cheese
½ cup grated Parmesan cheese
3 Tbsp. chopped fresh parsley
1 egg, beaten
½ tsp. salt
¼–½ tsp. pepper, according to your taste preference
6 cups spaghetti sauce
½ lb. mozzarella sauce, shredded

1. Prepare ziti according to package directions. Drain and set aside.

2. Brown ground beef. Stir frequently to break up clumps. Cook until pink no longer remains. Drain off drippings.

3. Stir in ricotta cheese, Parmesan cheese, parsley, egg, salt, and pepper.

4. Add spaghetti sauce. Stir until well mixed.

5. Add ziti. Toss gently to coat well.

6. Spoon into greased 9 × 13-inch baking pan.

7. Pour remaining spaghetti sauce over ziti mixture. Sprinkle with cheese.

8. Bake at 350°F for 45–60 minutes, or until bubbly and heated through.

Baked Ziti

Hope Comerford, Clinton Township, MI

Makes 8 servings

Prep. Time: 15 minutes ❧ *Cooking Time: 4 hours* ❧ *Ideal slow-cooker size: 5-qt.*

28-oz. can low-sodium crushed tomatoes

15-oz. can low-sodium tomato sauce

1½ tsp. Italian seasoning

1 tsp. garlic powder

1 tsp. onion powder

1 tsp. pepper

1 tsp. sea salt

1 lb. ziti or rigatoni pasta, uncooked, *divided*

1–2 cups low-fat shredded mozzarella cheese, *divided*

1. Spray crock with nonstick spray.

2. In a bowl, mix the crushed tomatoes, tomato sauce, Italian seasoning, garlic powder, onion powder, pepper, and salt.

3. In the bottom of the crock, pour ⅓ of the pasta sauce.

4. Add ½ of the pasta on top of the sauce.

5. Add another ⅓ of your pasta sauce.

6. Spread ½ of the mozzarella cheese on top of that.

7. Add the remaining pasta, the remaining sauce, and the remaining cheese on top of that.

8. Cover and cook on Low for 4 hours.

Mostaccioli

Sally Holzem, Schofield, WI

Makes 8 servings

Prep. Time: 45 minutes ⚶ *Baking Time: 30–45 minutes*

½ lb. bulk Italian sausage

½ cup chopped onion

16-oz. can tomato paste

½ cup water

½ tsp. oregano

¼ tsp. pepper

4-oz. can sliced mushrooms, drained

14½-oz. can diced tomatoes, undrained

¾ cup tomato juice

8-oz. pkg. mostaccioli noodles, *divided*

1½ cups cottage cheese

½ tsp. marjoram

12 oz. shredded mozzarella cheese, *divided*

¼ cup grated Parmesan cheese

1. Brown sausage and onion in saucepan, stirring often to break up clumps. When pink no longer remains, drain off drippings.

2. Stir in tomato paste, water, oregano, pepper, mushrooms, tomatoes, and tomato juice.

3. Cover. Simmer 30 minutes over medium heat.

4. Meanwhile, prepare noodles according to package directions. Drain well.

5. In mixing bowl, combine cottage cheese and marjoram.

6. In greased 7 × 13-inch baking pan, layer in half of noodles.

7. Top with half of meat sauce.

8. Sprinkle with half of mozzarella.

9. Spoon cottage cheese mixture over top and spread as well as you can.

10. Layer on remaining noodles.

11. Top with remaining meat sauce.

12. Sprinkle with remaining mozzarella cheese.

13. Sprinkle with Parmesan cheese.

14. Bake at 350°F for 30–45 minutes, or until bubbly, heated through, and lightly browned.

Pasta Pizza Pronto

Shari Jensen, Fountain, CO

Makes 6 servings

Prep. Time: 20 minutes & Baking Time: 37–40 minutes

Crust:

2 cups uncooked elbow macaroni

3 eggs

⅓ cup finely chopped onion

1 cup shredded cheddar cheese

Toppings:

1½ cups prepared pizza or pasta sauce

3-oz. pkg. sliced pepperoni

2¼-oz. can sliced olives, drained

1 cup sliced mushrooms, diced cooked ham or chicken, and/or diced bell peppers

1½ cups shredded mozzarella cheese

1. In a saucepan, cook macaroni according to package directions. Drain well.

2. In a large bowl, beat eggs. Stir in onion, cheddar cheese, and cooked macaroni.

3. Spread pasta mixture evenly on generously greased 14–16-inch pizza pan.

4. Bake at 375°F for 25 minutes on lower oven rack. Remove from oven.

5. Top with your favorite pizza or pasta sauce. Spread to within ½-inch of edge, using the back of a spoon.

6. Top evenly with pepperoni, olives, and 1 cup of the other toppings.

7. Finish by sprinkling with mozzarella cheese.

8. Return to oven and bake 12–15 minutes longer, until cheese is bubbly.

9. Remove from oven and slice with pizza cutter into 6–8 slices. Serve warm.

Tips:

1. Don't overload with toppings. Stay within the 1-cup suggestion.

2. Using the lower shelf of oven will crisp the crust. If not available in your oven, the middle shelf is okay.

3. Keep pasta pieces touching each other; no gaps.

Goulash

Janie Steele, Moore, OK

Makes 8–10 servings

Prep. Time: 15 minutes & Cooking Time: 6 hours & Ideal slow-cooker size: 5-qt.

1 lb. extra-lean ground beef
1 pkg. low-sodium taco seasoning
2 cups water
15-oz. can low-sodium diced tomatoes
15-oz. can low-sodium tomato sauce
15-oz. can whole-kernel corn, drained
Salt and pepper to taste
2 cups uncooked elbow macaroni

1. Brown meat in a skillet and drain.

2. Mix remaining ingredients except the macaroni together and pour into slow cooker.

3. Add elbow macaroni, then mix.

4. Cover and cook 6 hours on Low.

Ground Turkey Cacciatore Spaghetti

Maria Shevlin, Sicklerville, NJ

Makes 6 servings

Prep. Time: 15–20 minutes ♣ *Cooking Time: 5 minutes*

1 tsp. olive oil

1 medium sweet onion, chopped

3 cloves garlic, minced

1 lb. ground turkey

32-oz. jar spaghetti sauce, or 1 qt. homemade

1 tsp. salt

½ tsp. black pepper

½ tsp. oregano

½ tsp. dried basil

½ tsp. red pepper flakes

1 cup bell pepper strips, mixed colors if desired

1 cup diced mushrooms

13¼-oz. box Dreamfields spaghetti

3 cups chicken bone broth

1. Press the Sauté button on the Instant Pot and add the oil, onion, and garlic to the inner pot.

2. Add in the ground turkey and break it up a little while it browns.

3. Once ground turkey is browned, add in the sauce and seasonings.

4. Add in the bell peppers and mushrooms and give it a stir to mix.

5. Add in the spaghetti—break it in half in order for it to fit.

6. Add in the chicken bone broth.

7. Lock lid, make sure the vent is at sealing, and set on Manual at high pressure for 6 minutes.

8. When cook time is up, manually release the pressure.

Serving suggestion:
Top with some fresh grated Parmesan cheese and basil.

Mexi-Chicken Rotini

Jane Geigley, Lancaster, PA

Makes 6 servings

Prep. Time: 30 minutes   *Cooking Time: 4½ hours*   *Ideal slow-cooker size: 4-qt.*

1 cup water

3 cups partially cooked rotini

12-oz. pkg. frozen mixed vegetables

10-oz. can Ro-Tel diced tomatoes with green chilies

4-oz. can green chilies, undrained

4 cups shredded cooked chicken

1 cup low-fat shredded cheddar cheese

1. Combine all ingredients in slow cooker except shredded cheddar.

2. Cover and cook on Low for 4 hours.

3. Top with shredded cheddar, then let cook covered an additional 20 minutes or so, or until cheese is melted.

Turkey Tetrazzini

Hope Comerford, Clinton Township, MI

Makes 6–8 servings

Prep. Time: 10 minutes ♣ *Cook Time: 3 minutes*

2 Tbsp. butter

1 cup chopped onion

1 cup sliced mushrooms

3 cups chicken broth, *divided*

12 oz. wide egg noodles

2 cups chopped leftover turkey

1 cup frozen peas

½ tsp. salt

⅛ tsp. pepper

1 cup half-and-half

1½ cups shredded mozzarella cheese

½ cup grated or shredded Parmesan cheese

1. Set the Instant Pot to the Sauté function. Add the butter.

2. Sauté the onion and mushrooms in the melted butter for 2 to 3 minutes.

3. Pour in 1 cup of the chicken broth and scrape the bottom of the pot with a wooden spoon or spatula. Press Cancel.

4. Evenly spread the egg noodles around the Instant Pot, not stirring. Just press. Layer the turkey and peas over the top of the noodles and sprinkle with salt and pepper. Pour the remaining 2 cups of broth over the top.

5. Secure the lid and set the vent to sealing. Manually set the cook time for 3 minutes.

6. When the cook time is over, manually release the pressure.

7. When the pin drops, remove the lid and add the half-and-half and both cheeses, then stir together.

8. Let it sit for a bit to thicken, then serve.

Southern Comfort Mac n' Cheese

SLOW COOKER

MarJanita Martin, Batesburg, SC

Makes 6–8 servings

Prep. Time: 15 minutes ⚬ Cooking Time: 4 hours ⚬ Ideal slow-cooker size: 6–7 qt.

2 cups uncooked elbow macaroni

2 Tbsp. butter, melted

2 cups shredded cheese

2 Tbsp. Italian seasoning

2 tsp. salt

4½ cups milk

1. In a large bowl mix together all the ingredients except the milk.

2. Pour into a greased slow cooker.

3. Pour the milk over top.

4. Cover and cook on Low for 4 hours.

Super Creamy Macaroni and Cheese

Jean Butzer, Batavia, NY
Arlene Leaman Kliewer, Lakewood, CO
Esther Burkholder, Millerstown, PA
Hazel Lightcap Propst, Oxford, PA
Karla Baer, North Lima, OH

Makes 8–10 servings

Prep. Time: 5–10 minutes & *Baking Time: 1 hour 20 minutes*

1-lb. uncooked elbow macaroni

4 cups shredded cheddar cheese, or
½ lb. cubed Velveeta cheese

2 (10¾-oz.) cans cheddar cheese or
cream of celery soup

3½ cups milk

1½ cups cooked ham, chopped, *optional*

1 tsp. salt, *optional*

¼ tsp. pepper, *optional*

1. Combine all ingredients in a buttered 3-qt. casserole or baking dish.

2. Cover and bake at 350°F for 1 hour.

3. Stir up from bottom.

4. Bake uncovered an additional 20 minutes.

Salads

BLT Salad

Bernadette Veenstra, Grand Rapids, MI

Makes 12–16 servings

Prep. Time: 30 minutes & *Cooking Time: 15 minutes*

16-oz. pkg. rigatoni or penne pasta
1 lb. sliced bacon
7-oz. bag fresh spinach, roughly chopped
1 pt. cherry tomatoes, quartered
1 tsp. salt
¼ tsp. black pepper
8 oz. mozzarella cheese, cubed, *optional*

1. Cook pasta according to package directions. Drain and rinse under cold water. Transfer to a large bowl.

2. Dice bacon into small pieces. Sauté over medium heat. Place bacon on paper towel–lined plate. Pour all drippings into a small bowl.

3. Return 1 Tbsp. drippings to skillet and heat. Stir spinach into hot drippings until it wilts, about 1 minute. Transfer spinach to pasta.

4. Add ½ Tbsp. drippings to skillet and heat. Stir tomatoes into drippings in skillet. Cook for 2 minutes. Transfer tomatoes to spinach and pasta and toss.

5. If pasta seems dry, add up to 1½ Tbsp. more of the drippings.

6. Add salt, pepper, bacon, and cheese if desired. Refrigerate until serving time.

Fiesta Chicken Salad

Liz Clapper, Lancaster, PA

Makes 4 main-dish servings

Prep. Time: 25 minutes   Cooking Time: 10 minutes

2 heads Bibb or red leaf lettuce, or a combination

I cup shredded carrots

I medium tomato, diced

2 green onions, chopped

I sweet red pepper

I Tbsp. olive oil

I cup thawed frozen corn

I tsp. chili powder

2 cups diced rotisserie chicken meat

½ cup shredded cheddar cheese

8 Tbsp. ranch dressing

2 pita breads, 4-inch diameter, or flour tortillas

1. Tear up heads of lettuce and toss together in a large bowl. Top with shredded carrots, diced tomato, and chopped green onions.

2. Meanwhile, dice red pepper. Toss with olive oil and cook in a medium skillet over medium heat for 2 minutes.

3. Add corn and chili powder and cook for 1 more minute.

4. Top salad with diced chicken.

5. Spoon corn and pepper mixture over the top.

6. Sprinkle with cheese. Drizzle each salad with 2 Tbsp. dressing.

7. Grill pitas or tortillas for 2–3 minutes each side. Cut into fourths. Serve 2 wedges with each individual salad.

Mexican Salad

Jan Pembleton, Arlington, TX

Makes 10 servings

Prep. Time: 20 minutes ⚜ *Cooking Time: 15 minutes* ⚜ *Cooling Time: 30 minutes*

I head lettuce
¾ lb. 93%-lean ground beef
2 tomatoes, chopped
16-oz. can kidney beans, drained
¾ cup freshly grated cheddar cheese
¼ cup diced onion
¼ cup sliced black olives, sliced
I avocado, diced
2 oz. taco chips, crushed

Sauce:
8 oz. fat-free Thousand Island dressing
I Tbsp. dry low-sodium taco seasoning
I Tbsp. hot sauce
I Tbsp. sugar

1. Wash lettuce and tear into bite-sized pieces.

2. Brown, drain, and cool ground meat.

3. Combine all salad ingredients except taco chips. Set aside.

4. Combine all sauce ingredients. Pour sauce over salad and toss thoroughly.

5. Immediately before serving, add taco chips.

Greek Pasta Salad

Edie Moran, West Babylon, NY
Judi Manos, West Islip, NY

Makes 8 servings

Prep. Time: 15 minutes ⚭ *Cooking Time for pasta: 15 minutes*

1 cup dry pasta

4 medium plum tomatoes, chopped

15-oz. can garbanzo beans, rinsed and drained

1 medium onion, chopped

6-oz. can pitted black olives, drained

4-oz. pkg. crumbled feta cheese

1 clove garlic, minced

½ cup olive oil

¼ cup lemon juice

1 tsp. salt

½ tsp. pepper

1. Cook the pasta according to package instructions, then rinse it and put in the refrigerator to cool.

2. In a large bowl, combine cooled pasta, tomatoes, garbanzo beans, onion, olives, feta cheese, and garlic.

3. In a small bowl, whisk together oil, lemon juice, salt, and pepper. Pour over salad and toss to coat.

4. Cover and chill in refrigerator. Stir before serving.

Summer Pasta Salad

Judy Govotsos, Frederick, MD

Makes 15–18 servings

Prep. Time: 8–10 minutes ♒ Cooking Time: 15 minutes

1 lb. uncooked penne or corkscrew pasta
1 yellow pepper, sliced
1 green pepper, sliced
1 red pepper, sliced
1 red onion, sliced
8 oz. crumbled feta cheese, *optional*
½ lb. pitted kalamata olives, *optional*
cherry tomatoes, *optional*
16-oz. bottle Caesar salad dressing
10-oz. pkg. chicken strips, cooked, *optional*

1. Cook pasta according to package directions. Drain.

2. In a large mixing bowl, combine all ingredients except salad dressing and chicken.

3. Pour dressing over pasta mixture. Toss.

4. Add chicken, if using, immediately before serving.

Variations:

1. Instead of yellow and red peppers, substitute 2 cups cut-up broccoli florets in Step 2.

2. Instead of feta cheese, use 1 cup shredded cheddar cheese.

Soups, Stews & Chilies

Slow Cooker Tomato Soup

Becky Fixel, Grosse Pointe Farms, MI

Makes 8 servings

Prep. Time: 15 minutes & *Cooking Time: 6 hours* & *Ideal slow-cooker size: 6-qt.*

6–8 cups chopped fresh tomatoes
1 medium onion, chopped
2 tsp. minced garlic
1 tsp. basil
½ tsp. pepper
½ tsp. sea salt
½ tsp. red pepper flakes
2 Tbsp. chicken bouillon
1 cup water
¾ cup fat-free half-and-half

1. Combine your tomatoes, onion, garlic, spices, chicken bouillon, and 1 cup of water in your slow cooker.

2. Cover and cook on Low for 6 hours.

3. Add in your ¾ cup fat-free half-and-half and combine all ingredients with an immersion blender. Serve hot.

Split Pea Soup

Judy Gascho, Woodburn, OR

Makes 3–4 servings

Prep. Time: 20 minutes & Cooking Time: 15 minutes

4 cups chicken broth

4 sprigs thyme

4 oz. ham, diced (about ⅓ cup)

2 Tbsp. butter

2 stalks celery

2 carrots

1 large leek

3 cloves garlic

1½ cups dried green split peas (about 12 ounces)

Salt and pepper to taste

1. Pour the broth into the inner pot of the Instant Pot and set to Sauté. Add the thyme, ham, and butter.

2. While the broth heats, chop the celery and cut the carrots into ½-inch-thick rounds. Halve the leek lengthwise and thinly slice and chop the garlic. Add the vegetables to the pot as you cut them. Rinse the split peas in a colander, discarding any small stones, then add to the pot.

3. Secure the lid, making sure the steam valve is in the sealing position. Set the cooker to Manual at high pressure for 15 minutes. When the time is up, carefully turn the steam valve to the venting position to release the pressure manually.

4. Turn off the Instant Pot. Remove the lid and stir the soup; discard the thyme sprigs.

5. Thin the soup with up to one cup water if needed (the soup will continue to thicken as it cools). Season with salt and pepper.

Creamy Broccoli Soup

SuAnne Burkholder, Millersburg, OH

Makes 3–4 servings

Prep. Time: 10–15 minutes   *Cooking Time: 15–20 minutes*

4 cups milk, *divided*

1 Tbsp. chicken-flavored soup base

1 Tbsp. water

1½ cups cut-up broccoli

2 Tbsp. cornstarch

Salt to taste

1. Heat 3 cups milk and chicken base in a stockpot over low heat until hot.

2. Meanwhile, place cut-up broccoli in a microwave-safe dish. Add 1 Tbsp. water. Cover. Microwave on High for 1½ minutes. Stir. Repeat until broccoli becomes bright green and just-tender. Be careful not to overcook it! Drain broccoli of liquid.

3. In a small bowl, or in a jar with a tight-fitting lid, mix 1 cup milk and cornstarch until smooth. Slowly add to hot milk mixture.

4. Simmer gently, stirring constantly. When slightly thickened, add broccoli and salt.

Creamy Potato Soup

Hope Comerford, Clinton Township, MI

Makes 6 servings

Prep. Time: 20 minutes ❧ Cooking Time: 8–10 hours ❧ Ideal slow-cooker size: 5-qt.

8–9 Idaho potatoes, chopped into bite-sized pieces

4½ cups low-sodium chicken broth or stock

½ cup low-fat milk

1 medium onion, chopped

2–4 carrots, chopped

1–2 stalks celery, chopped

3 green onions, chopped

8-oz. block reduced-fat cream cheese, chopped into cubes

¼ cup nonfat plain Greek yogurt

3 Tbsp. cornstarch

2 Tbsp. butter

2 tsp. garlic powder

1 tsp. onion powder

1½ tsp. pepper

1 tsp. salt

1. Place all ingredients into your crock and stir.

2. Cook on Low for 8–10 hours.

Tip:

Use an immersion blender or potato smasher to give your soup a smoother and creamier texture.

Serving suggestion:

Serve with fresh chopped chives or green onions on top and little bit of shredded cheese.

Baked Potato Soup

Flo Quint, Quinter, KS
Susan Nafziger, Canton, KS

Makes 6–8 servings

Prep. Time: 30 minutes ⚸ *Cooking Time: 15–20 minutes*

1½ sticks (12 Tbsp.) butter

⅔ cup flour

7 cups milk

4 cups baked potatoes (about 5 large potatoes), peeled and cubed

4 green onions, sliced thin

8–12 strips bacon (according to your taste preference), cooked and crumbled

1¼ cups shredded cheese

8 oz. sour cream, *optional*

¾ tsp. salt, *optional*

¼ tsp. pepper, *optional*

1. Melt butter in large stockpot. Add flour and stir until smooth over medium heat.

2. Add milk, stirring often until thickened. Be careful not to scorch.

3. Add potatoes and onions and bring to a boil. Reduce heat and simmer 5 minutes, stirring often.

4. Remove from heat and add bacon, cheese, and sour cream if desired. Stir until melted.

5. Add seasonings if desired and blend thoroughly.

Variation:

Instead of 7 cups milk, you can use 4 cups milk and 3 cups chicken broth.

The Best Bean and Ham Soup

Hope Comerford, Clinton Township, MI

Makes 8–10 servings

Prep. Time: 8 minutes 🍃 Soaking Time: 8 hours or overnight
Cooking Time: 8–12 hours 🍃 Ideal slow-cooker size: 7-qt.

1 lb. dry navy beans
1 meaty ham bone or shank
1 cup chopped onion
2 cloves garlic, minced
1 cup chopped celery
¼ cup chopped parsley
1 Tbsp. sea salt
1 tsp. pepper
1 tsp. nutmeg
1 tsp. oregano
1 tsp. basil
2 bay leaves
8 cups low-sodium chicken stock
6–8 cups water

1. Soak the navy beans in water for 8 hours. Make sure the water is at least 2–3 inches above the beans. Drain and rinse.

2. Place the ham bone in the bottom of the crock and pour all the remaining ingredients into the crock around it, ending with the water. You'll want to make sure you've covered the ham bone with water.

3. Cover and cook on Low for 8–12 hours. Remove bay leaves before serving.

Chicken Noodle Soup

Colleen Heatwole, Burton, MI

Makes 6–8 servings

Prep. Time: 15 minutes ⚭ *Cooking Time: 4 minutes*

2 Tbsp. butter

1 Tbsp. oil

1 medium onion, diced

2 large carrots, diced

3 ribs celery, diced

3 cloves garlic, minced

1 tsp. thyme

1 tsp. oregano

1 tsp. basil

8 cups chicken broth

2 cups cubed cooked chicken

8 oz. medium egg noodles

1 cup frozen peas (thaw while preparing soup)

Salt and pepper to taste

1. In the inner pot of the Instant Pot, melt the butter with oil on the Sauté function.

2. Add onion, carrots, and celery with large pinch of salt and continue cooking on sauté until soft, about 5 minutes, stirring frequently.

3. Add garlic, thyme, oregano, and basil and sauté an additional minute.

4. Add broth, cooked chicken, and noodles, stirring to combine all ingredients.

5. Put lid on the Instant Pot and set vent to sealing. Select Manual high pressure and add 4 minutes.

6. When time is up do a quick (manual) release of the pressure.

7. Add thawed peas, stir, adjust seasoning with salt and pepper, and serve.

Note:

You can also prepare chicken for this recipe in the Instant Pot, but usually for this recipe, I use leftovers.

Slow Cooker Chicken Noodle Soup

Jennifer J. Gehman, Harrisburg, PA

Makes 6–8 servings

Prep. Time: 5–10 minutes ⚶ *Cooking Time: 4–8 hours* ⚶ *Ideal slow-cooker size: 5-qt.*

2 cups uncooked cubed chicken, dark or white meat

15¼-oz. can corn, or 2 cups frozen corn

1 cup green beans, or peas*

10 cups low-sodium chicken broth

½ (12-oz.) pkg. dry kluski (or other very sturdy) noodles

1. Combine all ingredients except noodles in slow cooker.

2. Cover. Cook on High 4–6 hours or on Low 6–8 hours.

3. Two hours before end of cooking time, stir in noodles.

---

* If using green beans, stir in during Step 1. If using peas, stir into slow cooker just 20 minutes before end of cooking time.

Easy Chicken Tortilla Soup

Becky Harder, Monument, CO

Makes 6–8 servings

Prep. Time: 5–10 minutes ⚶ *Cooking Time: 8 hours* ⚶ *Ideal slow-cooker size: 4- to 5-qt.*

4 chicken breast halves

2 (15-oz.) cans black beans, undrained

2 (15-oz.) cans Mexican stewed tomatoes, or Ro-Tel tomatoes

1 cup salsa (mild, medium, or hot, whichever you prefer)

4-oz. can chopped green chilies

14½-oz. can tomato sauce

Tortilla chips

1. Combine all ingredients except tortilla chips in large slow cooker.

2. Cover. Cook on Low 8 hours.

3. Just before serving, remove chicken breasts and slice into bite-sized pieces. Stir into soup.

4. Put a handful of tortilla chips in each individual soup bowl. Ladle soup over chips. Top with shredded cheese.

Shredded Pork Tortilla Soup

Hope Comerford, Clinton Township, MI

Makes 6–8 servings

Prep. Time: 10 minutes   ⚬   Cooking Time: 8–10 hours   ⚬   Ideal slow-cooker size: 5-qt.

3 large tomatoes, chopped

I cup chopped red onion

I jalapeño, seeded and minced

1-lb. pork loin

2 tsp. cumin

2 tsp. chili powder

2 tsp. onion powder

2 tsp. garlic powder

2 tsp. lime juice

8 cups low-sodium chicken stock

Garnish, *optional:*

Fresh chopped cilantro

Tortilla chips

Avocado slices

Freshly grated Mexican cheese

1. In your crock, place the tomatoes, onion, and jalapeño.

2. Place the pork loin on top.

3. Add all the seasonings and lime juice, then pour in the chicken stock.

4. Cover and cook on Low for 8–10 hours.

5. Remove the pork and shred it between two forks. Place it back into the soup and stir.

6. Serve each bowl of soup with fresh chopped cilantro, tortilla chips, avocado slices, and freshly grated Mexican cheese, if desired . . . or any other garnishes you would like!

Tip:

If you don't have time for freshly chopped tomatoes, use a can of diced or chopped tomatoes.

Taco Bean Soup

Colleen Heatwole, Burton, MI

Makes 8–10 servings

Prep. Time: 20 minutes ⚬ *Cooking Time: 4–6 hours* ⚬ *Ideal slow-cooker size: 6-qt.*

1 lb. lean ground turkey

1 large onion, chopped

14-oz. can pinto beans, undrained

15-oz. can black beans, undrained

15-oz. can kidney beans, undrained

2 (14½-oz.) cans peeled and diced tomatoes or 1 qt. fresh tomatoes

15-oz. can low-sodium tomato sauce

4-oz. can diced green chilies

1 pkg. low-sodium taco seasoning

15-oz. can whole-kernel corn, undrained

1. Brown ground turkey and onion in skillet.

2. Place turkey mixture in slow cooker along with other ingredients.

3. Cook on Low 4–6 hours.

Tip:

Any beans can be used in this recipe. You can keep frozen beans that you have cooked on hand and just use a combination.

Serving suggestion:

Serve with sour cream, grated cheese, and tortilla chips.

Minestrone

Bernita Boyts, Shawnee Mission, KS

Makes 8–10 servings

Prep. Time: 15 minutes ❧ *Cooking Time: 4–9 hours* ❧ *Ideal slow-cooker size: 3½- to 4-qt.*

1 large onion, chopped

4 carrots, sliced

3 stalks celery, sliced

2 cloves garlic, minced

1 Tbsp. olive oil

6-oz. can tomato paste

2 cups low-sodium chicken, beef, or vegetable broth

24-oz. can pinto beans, drained, rinsed

10-oz. pkg. frozen green beans

2–3 cups chopped cabbage

1 medium zucchini, sliced

8 cups water

2 Tbsp. parsley

2 Tbsp. Italian seasoning

1 tsp. sea salt, or more to taste

½ tsp. pepper

¾ cup dry acini di pepe (small round pasta)

Grated Parmesan, or Asiago, cheese, *optional*

1. Sauté onion, carrots, celery, and garlic in oil in skillet until tender. Add to slow cooker.

2. Combine all other ingredients, except pasta and cheese, in slow cooker.

3. Cover. Cook 4–5 hours on High or 8–9 hours on Low.

4. Add pasta 1 hour before cooking is complete.

5. Top individual servings with cheese, if desired.

Fresh Vegetable Soup

Sandra Chang, Derwood, MD

Makes 4–6 servings

Prep. Time: 25–30 minutes ❧ *Cooking Time: 60–70 minutes* ❧ *Standing Time: 1 hour*

½ stick (4 Tbsp.) butter
½ cup diced celery
½ cup diced onion
½ cup small chunks of peeled carrots
½ cup chopped cabbage
½ cup diced zucchini
½ cup fresh or frozen whole kernel corn
½ cup fresh or frozen cut-up green beans
2 cups canned whole tomatoes
4 cups beef stock
2 Tbsp. sugar
Salt to taste
Pepper to taste
½ cup fresh or frozen petite peas

1. In 4-qt. saucepan, melt butter. Sauté celery, onion, carrots, cabbage, and zucchini in butter until vegetables are soft but not brown.

2. Add rest of ingredients, except ½ cup peas.

3. Simmer gently for 30–45 minutes, or until vegetables are cooked but not mushy.

4. Take pan off heat and stir in peas. Allow soup to stand for 1 hour before serving.

5. Reheat just until heated through and serve.

Quickie French Onion Soup

Mary Puskar, Forest Hill, MD

Makes 6–8 servings

Prep. Time: 5–10 minutes ❧ *Cooking Time: 1 hour*

½ stick (4 Tbsp.) butter

3–4 good-sized onions (enough to make 5 cups sliced onion)

¼ cup flour

6 cups beef broth, or 3 (14½-oz.) cans beef broth, or 6 cups water with 6 beef bouillon cubes

6–8 melba rounds, *optional*

2 cups grated mozzarella cheese, *optional*

1. Melt butter in a large saucepan.

2. Meanwhile, slice onions.

3. Sauté onions in butter. After they become tender, continue cooking over low heat so that they brown and deepen in flavor, up to 30 minutes.

4. Sprinkle with flour. Cook 2 minutes.

5. Stir in broth, or water and bouillon cubes. Cover.

6. Heat to boiling and simmer 20 minutes.

7. Ladle into individual serving bowls.

8. Top each with melba rounds and/or grated cheese if you wish. For extra beauty and flavor, broil until cheese melts, but first make sure that the soup bowls can withstand the broiler heat. They could crack.

Meatball Tortellini Soup

Lucille Amos, Greensboro, NC

Makes 4 servings

Prep. Time: 5 minutes   Cooking Time: 20–25 minutes

14-oz. can beef broth
12 frozen Italian meatballs
1 cup stewed tomatoes
11-oz. can Mexican-style corn, drained
1 cup (20) frozen cheese tortellini

1. Bring broth to boil in a large stockpot

2. Add meatballs. Cover and reduce heat. Simmer 5 minutes.

3. Add tomatoes and corn. Cover and simmer 5 minutes more.

4. Add tortellini. Cover and simmer 5 more minutes, or until tortellini is tender.

Chicken Tortellini Soup

Mary Seielstad, Sparks, NV

Makes 4–6 servings

Prep. Time: 10–15 minutes & *Cooking Time: 25 minutes*

1 Tbsp. butter or margarine
4 cloves garlic, minced
5 cups chicken broth
9-oz. pkg. frozen cheese tortellini
1½ cups diced cooked chicken
14-oz. can stewed tomatoes
10-oz. pkg. frozen spinach
½ tsp. pepper
1 tsp. dried basil
¼ cup grated Parmesan cheese

1. In large saucepan, melt butter and sauté garlic for 2 minutes over medium heat.

2. Stir in broth and tortellini and bring to a boil. Cover, reduce heat, and simmer 5 minutes.

3. Add cooked chicken, tomatoes, frozen spinach, pepper, and basil and simmer 10–15 minutes. Stir every 3 minutes or so, breaking up frozen spinach and blending it into the soup.

4. Serve when soup is heated through, along with Parmesan cheese to spoon over individual servings.

Stuffed Sweet Pepper Soup

Moreen Weaver, Bath, NY

Makes 10 servings

Prep. Time: 20 minutes ❧ Cooking Time: 1 hour

1 lb. 95%-lean ground beef

2 qt. low-sodium tomato juice

3 medium red or green bell peppers, diced

1½ cups chili sauce, no salt added

1 cup uncooked brown rice

2 celery ribs, diced

1 large onion, diced

3 low-sodium chicken bouillon cubes

2 cloves garlic, minced

1. In large kettle over medium heat, cook beef until no longer pink. Drain off drippings.

2. Add remaining ingredients. Bring to a boil.

3. Reduce heat. Simmer, uncovered, for 1 hour, or until rice is tender.

Beef Barley Soup

Stacie Skelly, Millersville, PA

Makes 8–10 servings

Prep. Time: 15 minutes ⚘ *Cooking Time: 9¼–11½ hours* ⚘ *Ideal slow-cooker size: 6-qt.*

3–4-lb. chuck roast

2 cups carrots, chopped

6 cups low-sodium vegetable or tomato juice, *divided*

2 cups quick-cook barley

Water, to desired consistency

Salt and pepper to taste, *optional*

1. Place roast, carrots, and 4 cups juice in the slow cooker.

2. Cover and cook on Low 8–10 hours.

3. Remove roast. Place on platter and cover with foil to keep warm.

4. Meanwhile, add barley to the slow cooker. Stir well. Turn heat to High and cook 45 minutes to 1 hour, until barley is tender.

5. While barley is cooking, cut meat into bite-sized pieces.

6. When barley is tender, return chopped beef to the slow cooker. Add 2 cups juice, water if you wish, and salt and pepper, if you want. Cook for 30 minutes on High, or until soup is heated through.

Hearty Beef Stew

Hope Comerford, Clinton Township, MI

Makes 6–8 servings

Prep. Time: 30 minutes & Cooking Time: about 2 hours

1 ½ lb. stew beef

1 Tbsp. olive oil

4–5 carrots, chopped

4 stalks celery, chopped

1 large onion, chopped

4 small- or medium-sized potatoes, diced

14½-oz. can diced tomatoes

6-oz. can tomato paste

7 cups beef stock

1 tsp. onion powder

1 tsp. salt

1 tsp. pepper

1 tsp. oregano

2 bay leaves

1. Lightly brown the stew beef in 1 Tbsp. olive oil in the bottom of a stew pot.

2. Add in the carrots, celery, and onion and cook until the onion is translucent.

3. Add in the potatoes, diced tomatoes, tomato paste, beef stock, onion powder, salt, pepper, oregano, and bay leaves. Stir well.

4. Bring to a boil.

5. Reduce to a simmer and cover. Cook for an additional 2 hours. Remove bay leaves before serving.

Slow-Cooker Beef Stew

Becky Fixel, Grosse Pointe Farms, MI

Makes 8–10 servings

Prep. Time: 30 minutes ♣ *Cooking Time: 6 hours* ♣ *Ideal slow-cooker size: 3-qt.*

2 lb. cubed stew beef

¼ cup white rice flour

1½ tsp. salt

½ tsp. black pepper

32 oz. beef broth

1 onion, diced

1 tsp. Worcestershire sauce

1 bay leaf

1 tsp. paprika

4 carrots, sliced

3 potatoes, sliced thinly

1 stalk celery, sliced

1. Place the meat in crock.

2. Mix the flour, salt, and pepper. Pour over the meat and mix well. Make sure to cover the meat with flour.

3. Add broth to the crock and stir well.

4. Add remaining ingredients and stir to mix well.

5. Cook on High for at least 5 hours, then on Low for 1 hour. Remove bay leaf and serve.

Meme's Meatball Stew

Maxine Phaneuf, Washington, MI

Makes 6–8 servings

Prep. Time: 10 minutes   Cooking Time: 15 minutes

Meatballs:

1½ lb. lean ground beef

1 pkg. onion soup mix

¾ cup Italian bread crumbs

1 egg

Stew:

7 cups water

11¾-oz. can condensed tomato soup

2½ carrots, peeled and chopped

2 potatoes, peeled and chopped

2 big handfuls of fresh green beans, chopped

1 medium onion, chopped

1–2 tsp. salt

½ tsp. pepper

2 tsp. onion powder

2 tsp. garlic powder

1. In a medium bowl, mix the meatball ingredients and form into golf ball–size meatballs.

2. In the inner pot of the Instant Pot, add the stew ingredients. Carefully drop in the meatballs.

3. Secure the lid and set the vent to sealing. Manually set the cook time for 15 minutes on high pressure.

4. When the cook time is over, let the pressure release naturally for 10 minutes, then manually release the remaining pressure.

Serving suggestion:

Serve each bowl with grated Parmesan cheese and a side of crusty Italian bread with butter.

Quick and Easy Chili

Carolyn Spohn, Shawnee, KS

Makes 3–4 servings

Prep. Time: 10 minutes ☙ *Cooking Time: 25 minutes*

½ lb. ground beef, or turkey, browned and drained

1 medium-sized onion, chopped

2 cloves garlic, minced

2 (15-oz.) cans chili-style beans with liquid

8-oz. can tomato sauce

1. Brown ground beef in a large skillet.

2. Drain, leaving about 1 tsp. drippings in pan. Sauté onion and garlic until softened.

3. Add beans, with liquid, and the tomato sauce. Bring to a slow boil.

4. Reduce heat to simmer and cook for 15 minutes.

5. Return meat to skillet. Heat together for 5 minutes.

Tip:

Leftovers make good chili dogs.

Our Favorite Chili

SLOW COOKER

Ruth Shank, Gridley, IL

Makes 10–12 servings

Prep. Time: 20 minutes ❧ *Cooking Time: 4–10 hours* ❧ *Ideal slow-cooker size: 5-qt.*

1½ lb. extra-lean ground beef

¼ cup chopped onion

1 stalk celery, chopped

Extra-virgin olive oil, *optional*

29-oz. can stewed tomatoes

2 (15½-oz.) cans red kidney beans, drained, rinsed

2 (16-oz.) cans chili beans, undrained

½ cup ketchup

1½ tsp. lemon juice

2 tsp. vinegar

1 tsp. brown sugar

1½ tsp. kosher salt

1 tsp. Worcestershire sauce

½ tsp. garlic powder

½ tsp. dry mustard powder

1 Tbsp. chili powder

2 (6-oz.) cans tomato paste

1. Brown ground beef, onion, and celery in oil (if using) in skillet. Stir frequently to break up clumps of meat. When meat is no longer pink, drain off drippings.

2. Place meat and vegetables in slow cooker. Add all remaining ingredients. Mix well.

3. Cover. Cook on Low 8–10 hours or on High 4–5 hours.

Southwestern Chili

Colleen Heatwole, Burton, MI

Makes 12 servings

Prep. Time: 30 minutes ♣ *Cooking Time: 6–8 hours* ♣ *Ideal slow-cooker size: 6- or 7-qt.*

32-oz. can whole tomatoes

15-oz. jar salsa

15-oz. can low-sodium chicken broth

1 cup barley

3 cups water

1 tsp. chili powder

1 tsp. ground cumin

15-oz. can black beans

15-oz. can whole kernel corn

3 cups chopped cooked chicken

1 cup low-fat shredded cheddar cheese, *optional*

Low-fat sour cream, *optional*

1. Combine all ingredients in slow cooker except for cheese and sour cream.

2. Cover and cook on Low for 6–8 hours.

3. Serve with cheese and sour cream on each bowl, if desired.

Three-Bean Chili

Deb Kepiro, Strasburg, PA

Makes 6 servings

Prep. Time: 15 minutes   Cooking Time: 30–60 minutes

1 large onion, chopped

2 Tbsp. oil

2 cups diced cooked chicken

15½-oz. can kidney beans, rinsed and drained

15½-oz. can pinto beans, rinsed and drained

15½-oz. can black beans, rinsed and drained

2 (14½-oz.) cans diced tomatoes

1 cup chicken broth

¾ cup salsa

1 tsp. cumin

¼ tsp. salt

Shredded cheese, *optional*

Green onions, *optional*

Sour cream, *optional*

1. In a soup pot, sauté onion in oil until tender.

2. Add chicken, beans, tomatoes, broth, salsa, cumin, and salt.

3. Bring to a boil. Cover. Reduce heat and let simmer for 30–60 minutes.

4. If desired, garnish with shredded cheese, green onions, and sour cream.

Variation:

Add 1 cup corn, 1 Tbsp. chili powder, and 15½-oz. can undrained chili beans. Use 1 lb. ground beef, browned, instead of chicken.

—Moreen Weaver, Bath, NY

White Chicken Chili

Judy Gascho, Woodburn, OR

Makes 6 servings

Prep. Time: 20 minutes ♣ *Cooking Time: 30 minutes*

2 Tbsp. cooking oil

1½–2 lb. boneless chicken breasts or thighs

1 medium onion, chopped

3 cloves garlic, minced

2 cups chicken broth

3 (15-oz.) cans great northern beans, undrained

15-oz. can white corn, drained

4½-oz. can chopped green chilies, undrained

1 tsp. cumin

½ tsp. ground oregano

1 cup sour cream

1½ cups grated cheddar or Mexican blend cheese

1. Set Instant Pot to Sauté and allow the inner pot to get hot.

2. Add oil and chicken. Brown chicken on both sides.

3. Add onion, garlic, chicken broth, undrained beans, drained corn, undrained green chilies, cumin, and oregano.

4. Place lid on and close valve to sealing.

5. Set to Bean/Chili for 30 minutes.

6. Let pressure release naturally for 15 minutes before carefully releasing any remaining steam.

7. Remove chicken and shred.

8. Put chicken, sour cream, and cheese in the inner pot. Stir until cheese is melted.

Serving suggestion:

Can serve with chopped cilantro and additional cheese.

Desserts

Lemon Squares

Mary Kathryn Yoder, Harrisonville, MO

Makes 15 servings

Prep. Time: 10 minutes ⚭ *Baking Time: 30 minutes* ⚭ *Cooling Time: 1–2 hours*

1 box angel food cake mix
21-oz. can lemon pie filling
⅛ cup confectioners' sugar

1. Mix cake mix and pie filling together with an electric mixer.

2. Pour into a lightly greased 9 × 13-inch baking pan.

3. Bake at 350°F for 30 minutes. Let cool.

4. Sprinkle confectioners' sugar over top.

5. Cut into bars.

Cheesecake

Dot Hess, Willow Street, PA

Makes 12 servings

Prep. Time: 30 minutes   ⚓   *Baking Time: 1 hour 10 minutes*   ⚓   *Chilling Time: 3 hours*

Crust:

1½ cups crushed graham crackers

¼ cup sugar

½ stick (4 Tbsp.) butter, softened

Filling:

3 (8-oz.) pkgs. cream cheese, softened

5 eggs

1 cup sugar

1½ tsp. vanilla extract

Topping:

1½ pts. sour cream

⅓ cup sugar

1½ tsp. vanilla extract

1. Combine graham crackers, sugar, and butter. Press into bottom of 9-inch springform pan.

2. Beat cream cheese well with mixer. Add eggs, one at a time, mixing well after each one.

3. Add sugar and vanilla. Mix well.

4. Pour gently over prepared crust.

5. Bake at 300°F for 1 hour. Cool 5 minutes. Do not turn off oven.

6. As the cake cools, mix sour cream, sugar, and vanilla.

7. Spread topping on cake and bake 5 minutes more.

8. Chill for at least 3 hours before serving.

Variation:

Omit crust. Bake at 350°F for 35 minutes and proceed with topping.

—Renee Hankins, Narvon, PA

No-Bake Raspberry Cheesecake

Arlene M. Kopp, Lineboro, MD

Makes 10–12 servings

Prep. Time: 30 minutes   Chilling Time: 4–5 hours

3-oz. pkg. raspberry gelatin
1 cup boiling water
8-oz. pkg. cream cheese, softened
1 cup sugar
1 tsp. vanilla extract
1⅓ cups (19–20 crackers) graham cracker crumbs
¼ cup melted butter
3 Tbsp. lemon juice
12-oz. can evaporated milk, chilled

1. Place a large mixing bowl in the fridge. (You'll need it later to whip the milk.)

2. Combine gelatin and boiling water in a small bowl, stirring until gelatin is dissolved. Cool.

3. In a medium-sized mixing bowl, cream together cream cheese, sugar, and vanilla. Mix well.

4. Add gelatin. Mix well. Chill until it begins to set.

5. Meanwhile, combine cracker crumbs and butter in a small bowl. Press ⅔ of crumbs into the bottom of a 9 × 13-inch pan.

6. Combine lemon juice and milk in the bowl you've been chilling. Whip until it is stiff and holds a peak.

7. Lightly fold gelatin mixture into whipped mixture.

8. Pour into crumb crust in pan, being careful not to disturb the crumbs. Sprinkle top with remaining crumbs.

9. Chill until set, about 2–3 hours.

Chocolate Chip Cookies

Mary Martins, Fairbank, IA

Makes 3 dozen big cookies

Prep. Time: 15 minutes ⚜ *Chilling Time: 1 hour* ⚜ *Baking Time: 9 minutes per sheet*

2 sticks (16 Tbsp.) butter, at room temperature

1 cup brown sugar

1 cup sugar

3 eggs, beaten

3½ cups flour

2 tsp. cream of tartar

2 tsp. baking soda

½ tsp. salt

1 tsp. vanilla extract

12-oz. pkg. chocolate chips

1 cup chopped nuts, *optional*

1. In a large mixing bowl, combine butter, sugars, and eggs.

2. In a separate mixing bowl, sift together flour, cream of tartar, baking soda, and salt.

3. Add about one-third of the dry ingredients to the creamed mixture. Mix well. Add half of the remaining dry ingredients and mix well. Add the remaining dry ingredients and mix until thoroughly blended.

4. Stir in vanilla, chocolate chips, and nuts (if using). Chill in the fridge for 60 minutes.

5. Drop by spoonfuls onto a greased cookie sheet.

6. Bake at 400°F for about 9 minutes, or until lightly browned.

Tip:

1. If you like smaller cookies, make the spoonfuls in Step 5 about the size of a level teaspoon.

2. I usually bake a cookie sheet full and then cover the rest of the dough and keep it in the refrigerator for a day or so, so that I can have freshly baked cookies.

3. Use macadamia nuts in Step 4 for a real treat.

—Barb Yoder, Angola, IN

No-Bake Chocolate Cookies

Penny Blosser, Beavercreek, OH

Makes 36 cookies

Prep. Time: 20 minutes ♣ *Cooking Time: 15 minutes* ♣ *Cooling Time: 30 minutes*

½ cup tub margarine
½ cup milk
I cup Splenda® Sugar Blend
I cup chocolate chips
½ cup peanut butter
I tsp. vanilla extract
3 cups quick oats

1. Put margarine, milk, Splenda, and chocolate chips in a saucepan.

2. Bring to boil, and boil 1 minute. Remove from heat.

3. Stir in peanut butter and vanilla until melted.

4. Add rolled oats. Mix.

5. Drop by heaping tablespoonfuls onto waxed paper–lined baking sheet.

6. Let cool until set.

Peanut Butter Cookies

OVEN

Juanita Lyndaker, Croghan, NY
Stacy Stoltzfus, Grantham, PA
Joleen Albrecht, Gladstone, MI
Doris Bachman, Putnam, IL

Makes 1–1½ dozen cookies

Prep. Time: 15 minutes & *Baking Time: 8–10 minutes per sheet*

1 cup peanut butter
1 cup sugar
1 egg
Additional sugar

1. Mix the first three ingredients together in a medium-sized mixing bowl.

2. Break dough off with a teaspoon and shape into balls.

3. Roll each ball in granulated sugar.

4. Place on greased baking sheet. Press down with a fork, making a crisscross pattern.

5. Bake at 350°F for 8–10 minutes, or until golden brown.

Chocolate Sheet Cake

Robin Schrock, Millersburg, OH

Makes 18 servings

Prep. Time: 30 minutes ⚜ Baking Time: 20 minutes ⚜ Cooling Time: 1½ hours

Cake:

2 sticks (16 Tbsp.) butter

5 Tbsp. unsweetened cocoa powder

1 cup water

2 eggs, beaten

1 Tbsp. vinegar

1 tsp. baking soda

1 tsp. baking powder

½ cup sour milk, or buttermilk

1 Tbsp. vanilla extract

2 cups sugar

2 cups flour

½ tsp. salt

Frosting:

1 stick (8 Tbsp.) butter

5 Tbsp. unsweetened cocoa powder

½ cup milk

1 tsp. vanilla extract

Confectioners' sugar (around 1 lb.)

1. To make cake, combine butter, cocoa powder, and water in a small saucepan. Bring to a rolling boil, stirring occasionally. Remove from heat and cool.

2. When cooled, pour slowly into mixing bowl. Add eggs, vinegar, baking soda, baking powder, sour milk, and vanilla. Mix well.

3. In a separate bowl, mix the sugar, flour, and salt. Add to liquid mixture and blend thoroughly.

4. Pour into a 13 × 16 × 1½-inch cake pan. Bake at 350°F for 20 minutes.

5. Allow cake to cool to room temperature.

6. When ready to ice, make frosting by combining butter, cocoa powder, and milk in the saucepan. Bring to a rolling boil.

7. When slightly cool, add vanilla. Gradually add confectioners' sugar, ½ cup at a time, beating to make a spreadable consistency.

8. Ice cooled cake with frosting.

Tip:

To make sour milk, stir together ½ cup milk and 2 teaspoons apple cider vinegar. Allow to sit for 5 minutes before using.

Whoopie Pie Cake

Sheila Plock, Boalsburg, PA

Makes 20–24 servings

Prep. Time: 20 minutes ⚬ *Cooking/Baking Time: 20–25 minutes* ⚬ *Cooling Time: 1 hour*

1 chocolate cake mix

1 extra egg

Filling:

1 stick (8 Tbsp.) margarine, softened

½ cup shortening

1 cup sugar

Pinch salt

1 tsp. vanilla extract

½ cup milk

4 Tbsp. flour

1. Mix cake mix as directed on package with the addition of one extra egg.

2. Grease one 9 × 13-inch pan. Pour in half the batter.

3. Line another 9 × 13-inch pan with waxed paper on the bottom and up the sides to use as handles after the cake is baked.

4. Pour the other half of the batter in the waxed paper pan.

5. Bake according to package directions, possibly decreasing baking time because the mix is halved per pan. Check for doneness by inserting toothpick near center of cake. If toothpick is clean, cake is done. Cool at least 1 hour.

6. Make the filling by creaming margarine, shortening, sugar, and pinch of salt in a medium mixing bowl.

7. Slowly add vanilla and milk.

8. Add flour, 1 Tbsp. at a time. Beat on high 5 minutes until sugar dissolves.

9. Spread filling on bottom cake layer in greased pan.

10. To make the top layer, lift the other cake out of pan with waxed paper. Remove waxed paper. Place cake layer on top of filling.

Chocolate Soufflé

SLOW COOKER

Rachel Yoder, Middlebury, IN

Makes 10–12 servings

Prep. Time: 5 minutes   Cooking Time: 6 hours   Ideal slow-cooker size: 6-qt.

18¼-oz. pkg. chocolate cake mix
½ cup vegetable oil
2 cups sour cream
4 eggs, beaten
3-oz. box instant chocolate pudding mix
1 cup chocolate chips, *optional*

1. Combine all ingredients in a large mixing bowl.

2. Spray interior of slow cooker with nonstick cooking spray. Pour soufflé mixture into cooker.

3. Cover and cook on Low for 6 hours. (Do not lift the lid until the end of the cooking time!)

4. Insert toothpick into center of cake to see if it comes out clean. If it does, the soufflé is finished. If it doesn't, continue cooking another 15 minutes. Check again. Repeat until it's finished cooking.

5. Serve warm from the cooker with ice cream or frozen yogurt.

Upside-Down Chocolate Pudding Cake

Sarah Herr, Goshen, IN

Makes 8 servings

Prep. Time: 15 minutes ⚬ *Cooking Time: 2–3 hours* ⚬ *Ideal slow-cooker size: 3½-qt.*

1 cup dry all-purpose baking mix

1 cup sugar, *divided*

3 Tbsp. unsweetened cocoa powder, plus ⅓ cup, *divided*

½ cup milk

1 tsp. vanilla extract

1⅔ cups hot water

1. Spray inside of slow cooker with nonstick cooking spray.

2. In a bowl, mix the baking mix, ½ cup sugar, 3 Tbsp. cocoa powder, milk, and vanilla. Spoon batter evenly into slow cooker.

3. In a clean bowl, mix remaining ½ cup sugar, ⅓ cup cocoa powder, and hot water together. Pour over batter in slow cooker. Do not stir.

4. Cover and cook on High 2–3 hours, or until toothpick inserted in center of cakey part comes out clean.

Tip:

The batter will rise to the top and turn into cake. Underneath will be a rich chocolate pudding.

Pineapple Upside-Down Cake

Vera M. Kuhns, Harrisonburg, VA

Makes 10 servings

Prep. Time: 20 minutes ⚬ *Cooking Time: 4–5 hours* ⚬ *Ideal slow-cooker size: 4-qt.*

8 Tbsp. (1 stick) butter, or margarine, melted

1 cup brown sugar

1 medium-sized can pineapple slices, drained, reserving juice

6–8 maraschino cherries

1 box dry yellow cake mix

1. Combine butter and brown sugar. Spread over bottom of well-greased cooker.

2. Add pineapple slices and place cherries in the center of each one.

3. Prepare cake batter according to package directions, using pineapple juice for part of liquid. Spoon cake batter into cooker over top of fruit.

4. Cover cooker with 2 tea towels and then with its own lid. Cook on High 1 hour, and then on Low 3–4 hours.

Dump Cake

Janie Steele, Moore, OK

Makes 8–10 servings

Prep. Time: 10 minutes 🍃 Cooking Time: 12 minutes

6 Tbsp. butter

1 box cake mix (I used spice)

2 (20-oz.) cans pie filling (I use apple)

1. Mix butter and dry cake mix in bowl. It will be clumpy.

2. Pour pie filling in the inner pot of the Instant Pot.

3. Pour the dry mix over top.

4. Secure lid and make sure vent is at sealing. Cook for 12 minutes on Manual mode at high pressure.

5. Release pressure manually when cook time is up and remove lid to prevent condensation from getting into cake.

6. Let stand 5–10 minutes.

Serving suggestion:
Serve with ice cream.

Blueberry Bliss Dump Cake

SLOW COOKER

Hope Comerford, Clinton Township, MI

Makes 8 servings

Prep. Time: 10 minutes ❧ *Cooking Time: 5–6 hours* ❧ *Ideal slow-cooker size: 3-qt.*

2 cups blueberries

2 Tbsp. orange zest

1 Tbsp. fresh orange juice

½ cup turbinado sugar

¼ cup cornstarch

15-oz. box gluten-free yellow cake mix

¼ cup softened coconut oil

4 Tbsp. (½ stick) butter, cut into slices

1. Spray crock with nonstick spray or line with parchment paper.

2. Dump blueberries, orange zest, orange juice, turbinado sugar, and cornstarch into crock and mix.

3. Pour yellow cake mix over the top of the contents of the crock.

4. Place the coconut oil and slices of butter all over the top of the cake mix.

5. Cover and secure paper towel under the lid to absorb the moisture. Cook on Low for 5–6 hours.

Cherry Berry Cobbler

Carol DiNuzzo, Latham, NY

Makes 6 servings

Prep. Time: 10 minutes & Baking Time: 30 minutes

21-oz. can cherry pie filling

10-oz. pkg. frozen red raspberries, thawed and drained

1 tsp. lemon juice

½ cup flour

¼ cup sugar

⅛ tsp. salt

½ stick (4 Tbsp.) butter

1. In a saucepan, combine pie filling, raspberries, and lemon juice. Bring to a boil over medium heat.

2. Turn into a greased 1-qt. casserole.

3. In a bowl, mix the flour, sugar, and salt. Cut in butter until crumbly. Sprinkle over fruit.

4. Serve warm (not hot), alone or over ice cream.

Peach Cobbler

Phyllis Good, Lancaster, PA

Makes 8 servings

Prep. Time: 20 minutes   ❧   *Cooking Time: 3–4 hours*   ❧   *Ideal slow-cooker size: 5-qt.*

3–4 cups sliced peaches
⅓ cup sugar
¼ cup brown sugar
Dash nutmeg
Dash cinnamon
1 stick (8 Tbsp.) butter
½ cup sugar
¾ cup flour
2 tsp. baking powder
¾ cup milk

1. Grease interior of slow-cooker crock.

2. In a good-sized bowl, mix together the peaches, ⅓ cup sugar, brown sugar, nutmeg, and cinnamon. Set aside to macerate.

3. Melt butter, or place in slow-cooker crock turned on High and let it melt there.

4. Meanwhile, stir together remaining ingredients in a bowl—½ cup sugar, flour, baking powder, and milk—until smooth.

5. When butter is melted, make sure it covers the bottom of the crock. Spoon batter evenly over butter in crock, but don't stir.

6. Spoon sugared peaches over batter.

7. Cover. Bake on High 3–4 hours, or until firm in middle and bubbly around the edges.

8. Uncover carefully so condensation from inside of lid doesn't drip on the cobbler. Remove crock from cooker.

Serving suggestion:
Serve warm with milk or ice cream.

Apple Crisp

Mary Jane Musser, Manheim, PA

Makes 6 servings

Prep. Time: 15–20 minutes ❧ *Cooking Time: 2–4 hours* ❧ *Ideal slow-cooker size: 3-qt.*

6 cups peeled, cored, and sliced cooking apples
½ cup dry quick oatmeal
½ cup brown sugar
½ cup flour
1 Tbsp. butter, softened
½ tsp. ground cinnamon

1. Place apples in slow cooker sprayed with nonfat cooking spray.

2. Combine remaining ingredients in mixing bowl until crumbly.

3. Sprinkle mixture over apples.

4. Cover. Cook on Low 4 hours or on High 2 hours.

Grandma's Apple Pie

Andrea Zuercher, Lawrence, KS

Makes 8 servings

Prep. Time: 30 minutes & Baking Time: 45 minutes

6 cups pared and sliced apples (about 6 medium-sized tart apples; Granny Smith work well)

6-oz. can frozen 100%-juice apple juice concentrate, thawed

1 ½ Tbsp. cornstarch

1 Tbsp. water

1 tsp. cinnamon

10-inch double pie crust, unbaked

3 Tbsp. butter, *optional*

1. Place sliced apples in saucepan with juice concentrate.

2. Bring to a boil. Reduce heat, and then simmer, covered, for 5 minutes.

3. In a small bowl, dissolve cornstarch in water.

4. Gently stir into the apples.

5. Bring to a boil. Reduce heat. Simmer, covered, for 10–15 minutes. Apples will begin to soften as mixture becomes thickened. Stir occasionally so it does not scorch.

6. Gently stir in cinnamon.

7. Fill bottom pie crust with apples.

8. Dot with butter if you wish.

9. Cover with top crust. Pinch crusts together. With a sharp knife, cut 6–8 steam vents across the top crust.

10. Place pie pan on a baking sheet in case the filling cooks out. Bake at 350°F for about 45 minutes, or until top crust is lightly browned.

Autumn Pear Pie

MarJanita Martin, Batesburg, SC

Makes 6–8 servings

Prep. Time: 15 minutes ⚘ *Baking Time: 65 minutes*

3 cups peeled, diced, ripe pears

½ cup sugar

1 egg, beaten

1 cup sour cream

1 tsp. vanilla extract

1 Tbsp. flour

Dash salt

1 unbaked pie shell

Topping:

½ cup sugar

⅓ cup flour

¼ cup melted butter

1. Gently fold together the pears, sugar, egg, sour cream, vanilla, flour, and salt.

2. Place unbaked pie shell in a pie dish.

3. Use a fork to prick a few holes in the shell.

4. Put mixture into the pie crust.

5. Bake at 350°F for 25 minutes.

6. Meanwhile, mix topping ingredients together.

7. When the 25 minutes is over, place the topping on the pie.

8. Bake the pie for 40 more minutes.

9. Refrigerate before serving.

Serving suggestion:
This is best served cold with a scoop of ice cream on top!

Fudge Sundae Pie

Deb Martin, Gap, PA

Makes 6 servings

Prep. Time: 30 minutes   Freezing Time: 2 hours

¼ cup plus 3 Tbsp. light corn syrup,
divided

2 Tbsp. brown sugar

3 Tbsp. butter or margarine

2½ cups crispy rice cereal

¼ cup peanut butter

¼ cup ice cream fudge sauce

1 qt. vanilla ice cream

1. Combine ¼ cup corn syrup, the brown sugar, and the butter in a medium saucepan.

2. Cook over low heat, stirring occasionally, until mixture begins to boil. Remove from heat.

3. Add the crispy rice cereal, stirring until well coated.

4. Press evenly into a 9-inch pie plate to form crust.

5. Stir together the peanut butter, fudge sauce, and 3 Tbsp. corn syrup.

6. Spread half the peanut butter mixture over the crust. Freeze until firm, 1 hour.

7. Allow the ice cream to soften slightly.

8. Spoon the ice cream into the frozen piecrust; spread evenly. Freeze until firm, 1 hour.

9. Let pie stand at room temperature for 10 minutes before cutting and serving.

10. Warm the other half of the peanut butter mixture and drizzle over the top.

Tip:

Add chopped peanuts to the top, or whipped topping and maraschino cherries. Use butterscotch topping as drizzle.

Instant Pot Rice Pudding

Janie Steele , Moore, OK

Makes 6–8 servings

Prep. Time: 5 minutes   Cook Time: 14 minutes

1 ½ Tbsp. butter
1 cup uncooked rice
½ cup sugar
1 cup water
2 cups milk (2% works best)
1 egg
¼ cup evaporated milk
½ tsp. vanilla extract
½ tsp. almond extract, *optional*
Nutmeg, *optional*
Cinnamon, *optional*

1. Set the instant pot to the Sauté function, then melt the butter in the inner pot. Once the butter is melted, stir in the rice, sugar, water, and milk. Press Cancel.

2. Secure the lid and make sure the vent is set to sealing. Manually set the cook time for 14 minutes on high pressure. Let the pressure release naturally when the cook time is over.

3. In a bowl, whisk together the egg and evaporated milk.

4. Add a spoonful of the rice mixture to the egg and milk mixture and stir.

5. Return all to the inner pot and stir in the vanilla and optional almond extract.

6. Use the Sauté function and bring mixture to bubble for 30 to 60 seconds.

7. Stir slowly so it does not stick to the pot.

8. Use nutmeg or cinnamon to garnish if desired.

Mama's Rice Pudding

Shari Jensen, Fountain, CO

Makes 4–6 servings

Prep. Time: 5 minutes ❧ *Cooking Time: 6–7 hours* ❧ *Ideal slow-cooker size: 4-qt.*

½ cup white rice, uncooked

½ cup sugar

I tsp. vanilla extract

I tsp. lemon extract

I cup plus 2 Tbsp. milk

I tsp. butter

2 eggs, beaten

I tsp. cinnamon

½ cup raisins

I cup whipping cream, whipped

Nutmeg

1. Combine all ingredients except whipped cream and nutmeg in slow cooker. Stir well.

2. Cover pot. Cook on Low 6–7 hours, until rice is tender and milk absorbed. Be sure to stir once every 2 hours during cooking.

3. Pour into bowl. Cover with plastic wrap and chill.

4. Before serving, fold in whipped cream and sprinkle with nutmeg.

Metric Equivalent Measurements

If you're accustomed to using metric measurements, I don't want you to be inconvenienced by the imperial measurements I use in this book.

Use this handy chart, too, to figure out the size of the slow cooker you'll need for each recipe.

Weight (Dry Ingredients)

1 oz		30 g
4 oz	¼ lb	120 g
8 oz	½ lb	240 g
12 oz	¾ lb	360 g
16 oz	1 lb	480 g
32 oz	2 lb	960 g

Slow Cooker Sizes

1-quart	0.96 l
2-quart	1.92 l
3-quart	2.88 l
4-quart	3.84 l
5-quart	4.80 l
6-quart	5.76 l
7-quart	6.72 l
8-quart	7.68 l

Volume (Liquid Ingredients)

½ tsp.		2 ml
1 tsp.		5 ml
1 Tbsp.	½ fl oz	15 ml
2 Tbsp.	1 fl oz	30 ml
¼ cup	2 fl oz	60 ml
⅓ cup	3 fl oz	80 ml
½ cup	4 fl oz	120 ml
⅔ cup	5 fl oz	160 ml
¾ cup	6 fl oz	180 ml
1 cup	8 fl oz	240 ml
1 pt	16 fl oz	480 ml
1 qt	32 fl oz	960 ml

Length

¼ in	6 mm
½ in	13 mm
¾ in	19 mm
1 in	25 mm
6 in	15 cm
12 in	30 cm

Index

A

A.1. sauce
    Italian Sausage Dinner, 41
allspice
    Flavorful Beef Stroganoff, 91
Apple Crisp, 179
apples
    Baked Oatmeal, 10
    dried
        Cranberry-Apple Stuffed Pork Loin, 35
    Grandma's Apple Pie, 180
Autumn Pear Pie, 181
avocado
    Mexican Salad, 117
    Shredded Pork Tortilla Soup, 135

B

bacon
    Baked Potato Soup, 128
    BLT Salad, 115
    Breakfast Pizza, 19
    Easter-Morning Breakfast Casserole, 13
    turkey
        Turkey Bacon, Spinach, and Gruyère Quiche, 21
Baked Chicken Fingers, 45
Baked Oatmeal, 10
Baked Potato Soup, 128
Baked Ziti, 100
Barbecued Chicken Pizza, 85
Barbecued Chicken Thighs, 44
Barbecued Spareribs, 39
barbecue sauce
    Barbecued Chicken Pizza, 85
    Glazed Barbecue Turkey Meatloaf, 73
barley
    Beef Barley Soup, 145
basil
    Baked Chicken Fingers, 45
    Best Bean and Ham Soup, 129
    Chicken Noodle Soup, 131
    Chicken Tortellini Soup, 143
    Country Gal's Chicken Pot Pie, 75
    Ground Turkey Cacciatore Spaghetti, 105
    Italian Frittata, 23
    Lasagna, 93
    Slow Cooker tomato Soup, 123
    Upside-Down Pizza, 69
BBQ Chicken Sandwiches, 59
beans
    black
        Easy Chicken Tortilla Soup, 133
        Mexican Chicken Stack, 65
        Southwestern Chili, 153
        Taco Bean Soup, 136
        Three-Bean Chili, 155
    chili
        Our Favorite Chili, 152
        Quick and Easy Chili, 151

garbanzo
    Greek Pasta Salad, 119
great northern
    White Chicken Chili, 156
green
    Fresh Vegetable Soup, 139
    Meme's Meatball Stew, 149
    Minestrone, 137
    Slow Cooker Chicken Noodle Soup, 132
Huevos Rancheros in Crock, 22
kidney
    Mexican Salad, 117
    Our Favorite Chili, 152
    Taco Bean Soup, 136
    Three-Bean Chili, 155
navy
    Best Bean and Ham Soup, 129
pinto
    Minestrone, 137
    Slow Cooker Burritos, 64
    Taco Bean Soup, 136
    Three-Bean Chili, 155
beef
    Barbecued Spareribs, 39
    Beef and Pepperoncini Hoagies, 56
    Convenient Slow-Cooker Lasagna, 96
    Crazy Crust Pizza, 83
    Fabulous Fajitas, 52
    Flavorful Beef Stroganoff, 91
    Goulash, 104
    Grandma's Best Meatloaf, 71
    Hearty Beef Stew, 147
    Hearty Pot Roast, 27
    Herby French Dip Sandwiches, 55
    Household-Size Ziti Bake, 99
    Instant Pot Boneless Short Ribs, 36
    Lasagna, 93
    Lasagna the Instant Pot Way, 95
    Meme's Meatball Stew, 149
    Mexican Pizza, 87
    Mexican Salad, 117
    Mississippi Pot Roast, 28
    Our Favorite Chili, 152
    Oven Enchiladas, 63
    Quick and Easy Chili, 151
    Shepherd's Pie, 67
    Sloppy Joes, 57
    Slow-Cooker Beef Stew, 148
    Slow-Cooker Beef Stroganoff, 92
    Smoky Brisket, 32
    Stuffed Green Peppers, 68
    Stuffed Sweet Pepper Soup, 144
    Taco Meatloaf, 72
    Upside-Down Pizza, 69
    Veggie and Beef Stir Fry, 51
    Walking Tacos, 60
Beef and Pepperoncini Hoagies, 56
Beef Barley Soup, 145

beer
    Mom's Beer Ribs, 37
bell pepper
    Chicken Fajita Pizza, 84
    Easter-Morning Breakfast Casserole, 13
    Easy Chicken Fajitas, 53
    Fabulous Fajitas, 52
    Ground Turkey Cacciatore Spaghetti, 105
    Italian Sausage and Sweet Pepper Hash, 18
    Italian Sausage Dinner, 41
    Mexican Chicken Stack, 65
    Overnight Breakfast Casserole, 14
    Sloppy Joes, 57
    Stuffed Green Peppers, 68
    Stuffed Sweet Pepper Soup, 144
    Summer Pasta Salad, 120
    Sweet and Sour Chicken, 48
    Upside-Down Pizza, 69
Best Bean and Ham Soup, 129
biscuits
    Caramel Rolls, 5
    Chicken and Biscuits, 77
    Crustless Chicken Pot Pie, 76
    Instant Pot Chicken and Dumplings, 79
BLT Salad, 115
Blueberry Bliss Dump Cake, 175
Blueberry French Toast, 9
bread
    BBQ Chicken Sandwiches, 59
    Beef and Pepperoncini Hoagies, 56
    Blueberry French Toast, 9
    Country Brunch, 15
    Easter-Morning Breakfast Casserole, 13
    Memaw's French Toast, 7
    Overnight Breakfast Casserole, 14
    Sloppy Joes, 57
breakfast
    Baked Oatmeal, 10
    Blueberry French Toast, 9
    Caramel Rolls, 5
    Country Brunch, 15
    Easter-Morning Breakfast Casserole, 13
    Fiesta Hashbrowns, 17
    Huevos Rancheros in Crock, 22
    Italian Frittata, 23
    Italian Sausage and Sweet Pepper Hash, 18
    Memaw's French Toast, 7
    Overnight Breakfast Casserole, 14
    Sticky Buns, 6
    Sunrise Baked Oatmeal, 11
    Turkey Bacon, Spinach, and Gruyère Quiche, 21
Breakfast Pizza, 19
broccoli
    Creamy Broccoli Soup, 125
    Veggie and Beef Stir Fry, 51
burritos
    Slow Cooker Burritos, 64

C
cabbage
    Fresh Vegetable Soup, 139
    Kielbasa and Cabbage, 40
    Minestrone, 137
Caesar dressing
    Summer Pasta Salad, 120

cake
    Blueberry Bliss Dump Cake, 175
    Cheesecake, 160
    Chocolate Sheet Cake, 167
    Dump Cake, 173
    Pineapple Upside-Down Cake, 172
    Upside-Down Chocolate Pudding Cake, 171
    Whoopie Pie Cake, 168
cake mix
    Chocolate Soufflé, 169
    Lemon Squares, 159
    Pineapple Upside-Down Cake, 172
    Whoopie Pie Cake, 168
Caramel Rolls, 5
Carnitas Tacos, 61
carrots
    Beef Barley Soup, 145
    Chicken Noodle Soup, 131
    Crustless Chicken Pot Pie, 76
    Fiesta Chicken Salad, 116
    Fresh Vegetable Soup, 139
    Hearty Pot Roast, 27
    Instant Pot Boneless Short Ribs, 36
    Instant Pot Chicken and Dumplings, 79
    Meme's Meatball Stew, 149
    Minestrone, 137
    Split Pea Soup, 124
casserole
    Easter-Morning Breakfast Casserole, 13
    Overnight Breakfast Casserole, 14
cereal
    cornflakes
        Country Brunch, 15
    rice
        Easter-Morning Breakfast Casserole, 13
        Fudge Sundae Pie, 183
cheese
    Baked Potato Soup, 128
    Carnitas Tacos, 61
    cheddar
        Breakfast Pizza, 19
        Country Brunch, 15
        Crazy Crust Pizza, 83
        Fiesta Chicken Salad, 116
        Mexican Pizza, 87
        Mexican Salad, 117
        Mexi-Chicken Rotini, 107
        Overnight Breakfast Casserole, 14
        Pasta Pizza Pronto, 103
        Shepherd's Pie, 67
        Southwestern Chili, 153
        Super Creamy Macaroni and Cheese, 111
    cottage
        Convenient Slow-Cooker Lasagna, 96
        Lasagna, 93
        Lasagna the Instant Pot Way, 95
        Mostaccioli, 101
    Country Gal's Chicken Pot Pie, 75
    Easter-Morning Breakfast Casserole, 13
    feta
        Greek Pasta Salad, 119
        Summer Pasta Salad, 120
    Gruyère
        Turkey Bacon, Spinach, and Gruyère Quiche, 21
    Mexican-blend

Huevos Rancheros in Crock, 22
Mexican Chicken Stack, 65
Oven Enchiladas, 63
Pork Chop Pizziola, 33
Shredded Pork Tortilla Soup, 135
White Chicken Chili, 156
Monterey Jack
    Breakfast Pizza, 19
    Chicken Fajita Pizza, 84
    Easy Chicken Fajitas, 53
    Fiesta Hashbrowns, 17
mozzarella
    Baked Ziti, 100
    Barbecued Chicken Pizza, 85
    BLT Salad, 115
    Convenient Slow-Cooker Lasagna, 96
    Country Brunch, 15
    Crazy Crust Pizza, 83
    Fresh Veggie Lasagna, 97
    Household-Size Ziti Bake, 99
    Lasagna, 93
    Lasagna the Instant Pot Way, 95
    Mexican Pizza, 87
    Mostaccioli, 101
    Pasta Pizza Pronto, 103
    Quickie French Onion Soup, 140
    Stuffed Green Peppers, 68
    Turkey Tetrazzini, 108
    Upside-Down Pizza, 69
Parmesan
    Baked Chicken Fingers, 45
    Chicken Parmesan, 47
    Chicken Tortellini Soup, 143
    Fresh Veggie Lasagna, 97
    Italian Frittata, 23
    Lasagna, 93
    Mostaccioli, 101
    Turkey Tetrazzini, 108
provolone
    Beef and Pepperoncini Hoagies, 56
ricotta
    Fresh Veggie Lasagna, 97
Romano
    Grandma's Best Meatloaf, 71
Southern Comfort Mac n' Cheese, 109
Swiss
    Italian Sausage and Sweet Pepper Hash, 18
Three-Bean Chili, 155
Velveeta
    Super Creamy Macaroni and Cheese, 111
Walking Tacos, 60
Cheesecake, 160
No-Bake Raspberry Cheesecake, 161
cherries
    maraschino
        Pineapple Upside-Down Cake, 172
Cherry Berry Cobbler, 176
chicken
    Baked Chicken Fingers, 45
    Barbecued Chicken Pizza, 85
    Barbecued Chicken Thighs, 44
    BBQ Chicken Sandwiches, 59
    Chicken and Biscuits, 77
    Chicken Baked with Red Onions, Potatoes, and Rosemary,
        43

Chicken Fajita Pizza, 84
Chicken Noodle Soup, 131
Chicken Parmesan, 47
Chicken Tortellini Soup, 143
Country Gal's Chicken Pot Pie, 75
Crustless Chicken Pot Pie, 76
Easy Chicken Fajitas, 53
Easy Chicken Tortilla Soup, 133
Fiesta Chicken Salad, 116
Instant Pot Chicken and Dumplings, 79
Mexican Chicken Stack, 65
Mexi-Chicken Rotini, 107
Slow Cooker Burritos, 64
Southwestern Chili, 153
Summer Pasta Salad, 120
Sweet and Sour Chicken, 48
Three-Bean Chili, 155
White Chicken Chili, 156
Chicken and Biscuits, 77
Chicken Baked with Red Onions, Potatoes, and Rosemary, 43
Chicken Fajita Pizza, 84
Chicken Noodle Soup, 131
Chicken Parmesan, 47
Chicken Tortellini Soup, 143
chili
    Our Favorite Chili, 152
    Quick and Easy Chili, 151
    Southwestern Chili, 153
    Three-Bean Chili, 155
    White Chicken Chili, 156
chili powder
    Chicken Fajita Pizza, 84
    Fiesta Chicken Salad, 116
    Salsa Verde Pork, 31
    Shredded Pork Tortilla Soup, 135
    Sloppy Joes, 57
    Slow Cooker Burritos, 64
    Taco Meatloaf, 72
    Walking Tacos, 60
chili sauce
    Smoky Brisket, 32
    Stuffed Sweet Pepper Soup, 144
Chocolate Chip Cookies, 163
chocolate chips
    Chocolate Soufflé, 169
    No-Bake Chocolate Cookies, 164
Chocolate Sheet Cake, 167
Chocolate Soufflé, 169
cilantro
    Barbecued Chicken Pizza, 85
    Carnitas Tacos, 61
    Mom's Beer Ribs, 37
    Shredded Pork Tortilla Soup, 135
cinnamon
    Apple Crisp, 179
    Baked Oatmeal, 10
    Caramel Rolls, 5
    Flavorful Beef Stroganoff, 91
    Grandma's Apple Pie, 180
    Instant Pot Rice Pudding, 184
    Mama's Rice Pudding, 185
    Memaw's French Toast, 7
    Peach Cobbler, 177
    Sticky Buns, 6
    Sunrise Baked Oatmeal, 11

cloves
    Barbecued Spareribs, 39
cobbler
    Cherry Berry Cobbler, 176
    Peach Cobbler, 177
cocoa
    Chocolate Sheet Cake, 167
    Upside-Down Chocolate Pudding Cake, 171
Convenient Slow-Cooker Lasagna, 96
cookies
    Chocolate Chip Cookies, 163
    No-Bake Chocolate Cookies, 164
    Peanut Butter Cookies, 165
corn
    Crustless Chicken Pot Pie, 76
    Fiesta Chicken Salad, 116
    Goulash, 104
    Meatball Tortellini Soup, 141
    Mexican Chicken Stack, 65
    Slow Cooker Burritos, 64
    Slow Cooker Chicken Noodle Soup, 132
    Southwestern Chili, 153
    Taco Bean Soup, 136
    White Chicken Chili, 156
Country Brunch, 15
Country Gal's Chicken Pot Pie, 75
cranberries
    Cranberry-Apple Stuffed Pork Loin, 35
    Cranberry-Apple Stuffed Pork Loin, 35
Crazy Crust Pizza, 83
cream cheese
    Blueberry French Toast, 9
    Cheesecake, 160
    Creamy Potato Soup, 127
    Mexican Chicken Stack, 65
    Mexican Pizza, 87
    No-Bake Raspberry Cheesecake, 161
    Slow-Cooker Beef Stroganoff, 92
cream of celery soup
    Super Creamy Macaroni and Cheese, 111
cream of chicken soup
    Crustless Chicken Pot Pie, 76
cream of mushroom soup
    Flavorful Beef Stroganoff, 91
cream of potato soup
    Chicken and Biscuits, 77
Creamy Broccoli Soup, 125
Creamy Potato Soup, 127
Crustless Chicken Pot Pie, 76
cucumbers
    Walking Tacos, 60
cumin
    BBQ Chicken Sandwiches, 59
    Mexican Chicken Stack, 65
    Salsa Verde Pork, 31
    Slow Cooker Burritos, 64
    Southwestern Chili, 153
    Three-Bean Chili, 155
    White Chicken Chili, 156

D
desserts
    Apple Crisp, 179
    Autumn Pear Pie, 181
    Blueberry Bliss Dump Cake, 175
    Cheesecake, 160
    Cherry Berry Cobbler, 176
    Chocolate Chip Cookies, 163
    Chocolate Sheet Cake, 167
    Chocolate Soufflé, 169
    Dump Cake, 173
    Fudge Sundae Pie, 183
    Grandma's Apple Pie, 180
    Lemon Squares, 159
    Mama's Rice Pudding, 185
    No-Bake Chocolate Cookies, 164
    No-Bake Raspberry Cheesecake, 161
    Peach Cobbler, 177
    Peanut Butter Cookies, 165
    Pineapple Upside-Down Cake, 172
    Upside-Down Chocolate Pudding Cake, 171
    Whoopie Pie Cake, 168
Doritos
    Walking Tacos, 60
Dump Cake, 173

E
Easter-Morning Breakfast Casserole, 13
Easy Chicken Fajitas, 53
Easy Chicken Tortilla Soup, 133
eggs
    Huevos Rancheros in Crock, 22
    Italian Frittata, 23
enchiladas
    Oven Enchiladas, 63

F
Fabulous Fajitas, 52
fajitas
    Chicken Fajita Pizza, 84
    Easy Chicken Fajitas, 53
    Fabulous Fajitas, 52
Fiesta Chicken, 116
Fiesta Hashbrowns, 17
Flavorful Beef Stroganoff, 91
French toast
    Blueberry French Toast, 9
    Memaw's French Toast, 7
Fresh Vegetable Soup, 139
Fresh Veggie Lasagna, 97
frittata
    Italian Frittata, 23
Fudge Sundae Pie, 183

G
garlic
    Beef and Pepperoncini Hoagies, 56
    Best Bean and Ham Soup, 129
    Chicken Baked with Red Onions, Potatoes, and Rosemary, 43
    Chicken Fajita Pizza, 84
    Chicken Noodle Soup, 131
    Chicken Tortellini Soup, 143
    Fabulous Fajitas, 52
    Grandma's Best Meatloaf, 71
    Greek Pasta Salad, 119
    Ground Turkey Cacciatore Spaghetti, 105
    Lasagna, 93
    Minestrone, 137
    Pork Chop Pizziola, 33
    Quick and Easy Chili, 151

Salsa Verde Pork, 31
Shepherd's Pie, 67
Slow Cooker tomato Soup, 123
Split Pea Soup, 124
Stuffed Sweet Pepper Soup, 144
Taco Meatloaf, 72
Walking Tacos, 60
White Chicken Chili, 156
ginger
    Savory Pork Roast, 29
Glazed Barbecue Turkey Meatloaf, 73
Goulash, 104
graham crackers
    Cheesecake, 160
    No-Bake Raspberry Cheesecake, 161
Grandma's Apple Pie, 180
Grandma's Best Meatloaf, 71
Greek Pasta Salad, 119
green chilies
    Easy Chicken Tortilla Soup, 133
    Mexi-Chicken Rotini, 107
    Slow Cooker Burritos, 64
    Taco Bean Soup, 136
    White Chicken Chili, 156
Ground Turkey Cacciatore Spaghetti, 105

H
ham
    Best Bean and Ham Soup, 129
    Country Brunch, 15
    Lancaster County Ham Balls, 49
    Super Creamy Macaroni and Cheese, 111
Hearty Beef Stew, 147
Hearty Pot Roast, 27
Herby French Dip Sandwiches, 55
hot sauce
    Mexican Salad, 117
Household-Size Ziti Bake, 99
Huevos Rancheros in Crock, 22

I
ice cream
    Fudge Sundae Pie, 183
instant pot
    Chicken Noodle Soup, 131
    Cranberry-Apple Stuffed Pork Loin, 35
    Crustless Chicken Pot Pie, 76
    Dump Cake, 173
    Ground Turkey Cacciatore Spaghetti, 105
    Instant Pot Boneless Short Ribs, 36
    Instant Pot Chicken and Dumplings, 79
    Instant Pot Rice Pudding, 184
    Lasagna the Instant Pot Way, 95
    Meme's Meatball Stew, 149
    Mississippi Pot Roast, 28
    Split Pea Soup, 124
    Turkey Tetrazzini, 108
    White Chicken Chili, 156
Instant Pot Boneless Short Ribs, 36
Instant Pot Chicken and Dumplings, 79
Instant Pot Rice Pudding, 184
Italian dressing
    Easy Chicken Fajitas, 53
Italian Frittata, 23
Italian Sausage and Sweet Pepper Hash, 18

Italian Sausage Dinner, 41
Italian seasoning
    Baked Ziti, 100
    Country Gal's Chicken Pot Pie, 75
    Glazed Barbecue Turkey Meatloaf, 73
    Lasagna the Instant Pot Way, 95
    Minestrone, 137
    Pork Chop Pizziola, 33
    Southern Comfort Mac n' Cheese, 109

J
jalapeño
    Carnitas Tacos, 61
    Fiesta Hashbrowns, 17
    Shredded Pork Tortilla Soup, 135

K
ketchup
    Barbecued Chicken Thighs, 44
    BBQ Chicken Sandwiches, 59
    Grandma's Best Meatloaf, 71
    Sloppy Joes, 57
    Sweet and Sour Chicken, 48
Kielbasa and Cabbage, 40

L
Lancaster County Ham Balls, 49
Lasagna, 93
    Convenient Slow-Cooker Lasagna, 96
    Fresh Veggie Lasagna, 97
    Lasagna the Instant Pot Way, 95
Lasagna the Instant Pot Way, 95
leek
    Split Pea Soup, 124
Lemon Squares, 159
lettuce
    Fiesta Chicken Salad, 116
    Mexican Pizza, 87
    Mexican Salad, 117
    Walking Tacos, 60

M
mace
    Savory Pork Roast, 29
Mama's Rice Pudding, 185
marjoram
    Mostaccioli, 101
meatballs
    Meatball Tortellini Soup, 141
Meatball Tortellini Soup, 141
meatloaf
    Glazed Barbecue Turkey Meatloaf, 73
    Grandma's Best Meatloaf, 71
    Taco Meatloaf, 72
Memaw's French Toast, 7
Meme's Meatball Stew, 149
Mexican Chicken Stack, 65
Mexican Pizza, 87
Mexican Salad, 117
Mexi-Chicken Rotini, 107
Minestrone, 137
mint
    Italian Frittata, 23
Mississippi Pot Roast, 28
Mom's Beer Ribs, 37

Mostaccioli, 101
mushrooms
    Easter-Morning Breakfast Casserole, 13
    Flavorful Beef Stroganoff, 91
    Fresh Veggie Lasagna, 97
    Ground Turkey Cacciatore Spaghetti, 105
    Lasagna the Instant Pot Way, 95
    Mostaccioli, 101
    Overnight Breakfast Casserole, 14
    Pasta Pizza Pronto, 103
    Slow-Cooker Beef Stroganoff, 92
    Turkey Tetrazzini, 108
    Upside-Down Pizza, 69
mustard
    Cranberry-Apple Stuffed Pork Loin, 35
    Easter-Morning Breakfast Casserole, 13
    Lancaster County Ham Balls, 49
    Sloppy Joes, 57

N
No-Bake Chocolate Cookies, 164
No-Bake Raspberry Cheesecake, 161
noodles
    Chicken Noodle Soup, 131
    Convenient Slow-Cooker Lasagna, 96
    Flavorful Beef Stroganoff, 91
    Goulash, 104
    Lasagna, 93
    Lasagna the Instant Pot Way, 95
    Slow Cooker Chicken Noodle Soup, 132
    Southern Comfort Mac n' Cheese, 109
    Super Creamy Macaroni and Cheese, 111
    Turkey Tetrazzini, 108
nutmeg
    Baked Oatmeal, 10
    Instant Pot Rice Pudding, 184
    Memaw's French Toast, 7
    Peach Cobbler, 177
    Savory Pork Roast, 29

O
oats
    Apple Crisp, 179
    Baked Oatmeal, 10
    No-Bake Chocolate Cookies, 164
    Sunrise Baked Oatmeal, 11
olives
    Greek Pasta Salad, 119
    Mexican Pizza, 87
    Mexican Salad, 117
    Pasta Pizza Pronto, 103
    Pork Chop Pizziola, 33
    Summer Pasta Salad, 120
oregano
    Best Bean and Ham Soup, 129
    Carnitas Tacos, 61
    Chicken Noodle Soup, 131
    Crazy Crust Pizza, 83
    Fresh Veggie Lasagna, 97
    Ground Turkey Cacciatore Spaghetti, 105
    Hearty Beef Stew, 147
    Italian Frittata, 23
    Lasagna; 93
    Mostaccioli, 101
    Upside-Down Pizza, 69

    Walking Tacos, 60
    White Chicken Chili, 156
Our Favorite Chili, 152
Oven Enchiladas, 63
Overnight Breakfast Casserole, 14

P
paprika
    Carnitas Tacos, 61
    Slow-Cooker Beef Stew, 148
    Slow-Cooker Beef Stroganoff, 92
parsley
    Italian Sausage and Sweet Pepper Hash, 18
pasta
    Baked Ziti, 100
    BLT Salad, 115
    Chicken Tortellini Soup, 143
    Greek Pasta Salad, 119
    Ground Turkey Cacciatore Spaghetti, 105
    Household-Size Ziti Bake, 99
    Meatball Tortellini Soup, 141
    Mexi-Chicken Rotini, 107
    Minestrone, 137
    Mostaccioli, 101
    Pasta Pizza Pronto, 103
    Summer Pasta Salad, 120
Pasta Pizza Pronto, 103
Peach Cobbler, 177
peanut butter
    Fudge Sundae Pie, 183
Peanut Butter Cookies, 165
pears
    Autumn Pear Pie, 181
peas
    Chicken Noodle Soup, 131
    Crustless Chicken Pot Pie, 76
    Fresh Vegetable Soup, 139
    Slow Cooker Chicken Noodle Soup, 132
    split
        Split Pea Soup, 124
    Turkey Tetrazzini, 108
pepperoncini
    Mississippi Pot Roast, 28
    Pork Chop Pizziola, 33
pepperoni
    Pasta Pizza Pronto, 103
pie
    Autumn Pear Pie, 181
    Fudge Sundae Pie, 183
    Grandma's Apple Pie, 180
pie filling
    Cherry Berry Cobbler, 176
pineapple
    Carnitas Tacos, 61
Pineapple Upside-Down Cake, 172
pita
    Fiesta Chicken Salad, 116
pizza
    Barbecued Chicken Pizza, 85
    Breakfast Pizza, 19
    Chicken Fajita Pizza, 84
    Crazy Crust Pizza, 83
    Mexican Pizza, 87
    Upside-Down Pizza, 69
pork

Carnitas Tacos, 61
Cranberry-Apple Stuffed Pork Loin, 35
Mom's Beer Ribs, 37
Pork Chop Pizziola, 33
Salsa Verde Pork, 31
Savory Pork Roast, 29
Shredded Pork Tortilla Soup, 135
Taco Meatloaf, 72
Pork Chop Pizziola, 33
potatoes
Chicken Baked with Red Onions, Potatoes, and Rosemary, 43
Creamy Potato Soup, 127
hash browns
Fiesta Hashbrowns, 17
Hearty Beef Stew, 147
Hearty Pot Roast, 27
Italian Sausage and Sweet Pepper Hash, 18
Meme's Meatball Stew, 149
Mississippi Pot Roast, 28
Shepherd's Pie, 67
Slow-Cooker Beef Stew, 148
pot pie
Country Gal's Chicken Pot Pie, 75
Crustless Chicken Pot Pie, 76
pot roast
Hearty Pot Roast, 27
Mississippi Pot Roast, 28
prosciutto
Italian Frittata, 23
pudding mix
Chocolate Soufflé, 169

Q
Quick and Easy Chili, 151
Quickie French Onion Soup, 140

R
raisins
Baked Oatmeal, 10
Mama's Rice Pudding, 185
ranch dressing
Fiesta Chicken Salad, 116
raspberries
Cherry Berry Cobbler, 176
rice
brown
Slow Cooker Burritos, 64
Stuffed Sweet Pepper Soup, 144
Veggie and Beef Stir Fry, 51
Carnitas Tacos, 61
Italian Sausage Dinner, 41
Mama's Rice Pudding, 185
Stuffed Green Peppers, 68
Sweet and Sour Chicken, 48
rice pudding
Instant Pot Rice Pudding, 184
Mama's Rice Pudding, 185
rosemary
Chicken Baked with Red Onions, Potatoes, and Rosemary, 43
Country Gal's Chicken Pot Pie, 75
Cranberry-Apple Stuffed Pork Loin, 35
Herby French Dip Sandwiches, 55
Instant Pot Boneless Short Ribs, 36

Savory Pork Roast, 29

S
sage
Cranberry-Apple Stuffed Pork Loin, 35
Italian Frittata, 23
salad
BLT Salad, 115
Fiesta Chicken Salad, 116
Greek Pasta Salad, 119
Mexican Salad, 117
Summer Pasta Salad, 120
salsa
Carnitas Tacos, 61
Chicken Fajita Pizza, 84
Easy Chicken Fajitas, 53
Easy Chicken Tortilla Soup, 133
Huevos Rancheros in Crock, 22
Mexican Chicken Stack, 65
Salsa Verde Pork, 31
Slow Cooker Burritos, 64
Three-Bean Chili, 155
Walking Tacos, 60
Salsa Verde Pork, 31
sandwiches
BBQ Chicken Sandwiches, 59
Beef and Pepperoncini Hoagies, 56
Herby French Dip Sandwiches, 55
Sloppy Joes, 57
sausage
Country Brunch, 15
Crazy Crust Pizza, 83
Easter-Morning Breakfast Casserole, 13
Fiesta Hashbrowns, 17
Italian Sausage and Sweet Pepper Hash, 18
Italian Sausage Dinner, 41
Kielbasa and Cabbage, 40
Mostaccioli, 101
Overnight Breakfast Casserole, 14
Sloppy Joes, 57
Savory Pork Roast, 29
seafood
Shepherd's Pie, 67
Shredded Pork Tortilla Soup, 135
Sloppy Joes, 57
slow cooker
Apple Crisp, 179
Baked Ziti, 100
BBQ Chicken Sandwiches, 59
Beef and Pepperoncini Hoagies, 56
Beef Barley Soup, 145
Best Bean and Ham Soup, 129
Blueberry Bliss Dump Cake, 175
Carnitas Tacos, 61
Chicken and Biscuits, 77
Chocolate Soufflé, 169
Convenient Slow-Cooker Lasagna, 96
Creamy Potato Soup, 127
Easy Chicken Tortilla Soup, 133
Fabulous Fajitas, 52
Fiesta Hashbrowns, 17
Fresh Veggie Lasagna, 97
Glazed Barbecue Turkey Meatloaf, 73
Goulash, 104
Herby French Dip Sandwiches, 55

Huevos Rancheros in Crock, 22
Italian Frittata, 23
Italian Sausage and Sweet Pepper Hash, 18
Italian Sausage Dinner, 41
Kielbasa and Cabbage, 40
Lancaster County Ham Balls, 49
Mama's Rice Pudding, 185
Mexi-Chicken Rotini, 107
Minestrone, 137
Mom's Beer Ribs, 37
Our Favorite Chili, 152
Peach Cobbler, 177
Pineapple Upside-Down Cake, 172
Salsa Verde Pork, 31
Savory Pork Roast, 29
Shredded Pork Tortilla Soup, 135
Sloppy Joes, 57
Slow-Cooker Beef Stew, 148
Slow-Cooker Beef Stroganoff, 92
Slow Cooker Chicken Noodle Soup, 132
Slow Cooker tomato Soup, 123
Smoky Brisket, 32
Southern Comfort Mac n' Cheese, 109
Southwestern Chili, 153
Sweet and Sour Chicken, 48
Taco Bean Soup, 136
Taco Meatloaf, 72
Turkey Bacon, Spinach, and Gruyère Quiche, 21
Upside-Down Chocolate Pudding Cake, 171
Walking Tacos, 60
Slow-Cooker Beef Stew, 148
Slow-Cooker Beef Stroganoff, 92
Slow Cooker Burritos, 64
Slow Cooker Chicken Noodle Soup, 132
Slow Cooker tomato Soup, 123
Smoky Brisket, 32
soufflé
Chocolate Soufflé, 169
soup
Baked Potato Soup, 128
Beef Barley Soup, 145
Best Bean and Ham Soup, 129
Chicken Noodle Soup, 131
Chicken Tortellini Soup, 143
Creamy Broccoli Soup, 125
Creamy Potato Soup, 127
Easy Chicken Tortilla Soup, 133
Fresh Vegetable Soup, 139
Meatball Tortellini Soup, 141
Minestrone, 137
Quickie French Onion Soup, 140
Slow Cooker Chicken Noodle Soup, 132
Slow Cooker tomato Soup, 123
Split Pea Soup, 124
Stuffed Sweet Pepper Soup, 144
Taco Bean Soup, 136
Southern Comfort Mac n' Cheese, 109
Southwestern Chili, 153
soy sauce
Herby French Dip Sandwiches, 55
Sweet and Sour Chicken, 48
spinach
BLT Salad, 115
Chicken Tortellini Soup, 143
Fresh Veggie Lasagna, 97

Turkey Bacon, Spinach, and Gruyère Quiche, 21
Split Pea Soup, 124
squash
Veggie and Beef Stir Fry, 51
stew
Hearty Beef Stew, 147
Meme's Meatball Stew, 149
Slow-Cooker Beef Stew, 148
Sticky Buns, 6
stroganoff
Flavorful Beef Stroganoff, 91
Slow-Cooker Beef Stroganoff, 92
Stuffed Green Peppers, 68
Stuffed Sweet Pepper Soup, 144
Summer Pasta Salad, 120
Sunrise Baked Oatmeal, 11
Super Creamy Macaroni and Cheese, 111
Sweet and Sour Chicken, 48

T
Taco Bean Soup, 136
Taco Meatloaf, 72
tacos
Carnitas Tacos, 61
Walking Tacos, 60
taco seasoning
Taco Meatloaf, 72
tapioca
Fiesta Hashbrowns, 17
teriyaki sauce
Veggie and Beef Stir Fry, 51
Thousand Island dressing
Mexican Salad, 117
Three-Bean Chili, 155
thyme
Baked Chicken Fingers, 45
Chicken Noodle Soup, 131
Herby French Dip Sandwiches, 55
Instant Pot Boneless Short Ribs, 36
Italian Sausage and Sweet Pepper Hash, 18
Split Pea Soup, 124
tomatoes
Baked Ziti, 100
BLT Salad, 115
Chicken Tortellini Soup, 143
Easy Chicken Fajitas, 53
Easy Chicken Tortilla Soup, 133
Fiesta Chicken Salad, 116
Fresh Vegetable Soup, 139
Goulash, 104
Greek Pasta Salad, 119
Hearty Beef Stew, 147
Italian Sausage Dinner, 41
Kielbasa and Cabbage, 40
Lasagna, 93
Meatball Tortellini Soup, 141
Mexi-Chicken Rotini, 107
Mostaccioli, 101
Our Favorite Chili, 152
Overnight Breakfast Casserole, 14
Salsa Verde Pork, 31
Shredded Pork Tortilla Soup, 135
Slow Cooker tomato Soup, 123
Southwestern Chili, 153
Summer Pasta Salad, 120

Taco Bean Soup, 136
Taco Meatloaf, 72
Three-Bean Chili, 155
Walking Tacos, 60
tomato sauce
  Baked Ziti, 100
  Chicken Parmesan, 47
  Convenient Slow-Cooker Lasagna, 96
  Crazy Crust Pizza, 83
  Easy Chicken Tortilla Soup, 133
  Goulash, 104
  Ground Turkey Cacciatore Spaghetti, 105
  Household-Size Ziti Bake, 99
  Lasagna the Instant Pot Way, 95
  Pasta Pizza Pronto, 103
  Pork Chop Pizziola, 33
  Quick and Easy Chili, 151
  Sloppy Joes, 57
  Stuffed Green Peppers, 68
  Upside-Down Pizza, 69
tomato soup
  Barbecued Spareribs, 39
  Meme's Meatball Stew, 149
  Slow Cooker Tomato Soup, 123
tortellini
  Chicken Tortellini Soup, 143
  Meatball Tortellini Soup, 141
tortilla chips
  Taco Meatloaf, 72
tortillas
  Carnitas Tacos, 61
  Easy Chicken Fajitas, 53
  Fabulous Fajitas, 52
  Fiesta Chicken Salad, 116
  Huevos Rancheros in Crock, 22
  Mexican Chicken Stack, 65
  Oven Enchiladas, 63
  Slow Cooker Burritos, 64
turkey
  bacon
    Turkey Bacon, Spinach, and Gruyère Quiche, 21
  Glazed Barbecue Turkey Meatloaf, 73
  Ground Turkey Cacciatore Spaghetti, 105
  Quick and Easy Chili, 151
  sausage
    Fiesta Hashbrowns, 17
    Italian Sausage and Sweet Pepper Hash, 18
    Sloppy Joes, 57
  Taco Bean Soup, 136
Turkey Bacon, Spinach, and Gruyère Quiche, 21
Turkey Tetrazzini, 108

U
Upside-Down Chocolate Pudding Cake, 171
Upside-Down Pizza, 69

V
vegetarian
  Baked Oatmeal, 10
  Creamy Broccoli Soup, 125
  Creamy Potato Soup, 127
  Huevos Rancheros in Crock, 22
  Pasta Pizza Pronto, 103
  Quickie French Onion Soup, 140
  Southern Comfort Mac n' Cheese, 109
  Sunrise Baked Oatmeal, 11
Veggie and Beef Stir Fry, 51
vinegar
  apple cider
    Barbecued Chicken Thighs, 44
    BBQ Chicken Sandwiches, 59
    Sloppy Joes, 57
    Sweet and Sour Chicken, 48
  balsamic, 36
    Chicken Baked with Red Onions, Potatoes, and Rosemary, 43
    Instant Pot Boneless Short Ribs, 36

W
Walking Tacos, 60
White Chicken Chili, 156
Whoopie Pie Cake, 168
wine
  red
    Instant Pot Boneless Short Ribs, 36
  white
    Salsa Verde Pork, 31

Y
yogurt
  Creamy Potato Soup, 127
  Slow-Cooker Beef Stroganoff, 92

Z
zucchini
  Fresh Vegetable Soup, 139
  Fresh Veggie Lasagna, 97
  Minestrone, 137
  Veggie and Beef Stir Fry, 51

About the Author

Hope Comerford is a mom, wife, elementary music teacher, blogger, recipe developer, public speaker, Young Living Essential Oils essential oil enthusiast/educator, and published author. In 2013, she was diagnosed with a severe gluten intolerance and since then has spent many hours creating easy, practical, and delicious gluten-free recipes that can be enjoyed by both those who are affected by gluten and those who are not.

Growing up, Hope spent many hours in the kitchen with her meme (grandmother) and her love for cooking grew from there. While working on her master's degree when her daughter was young, Hope turned to her slow cookers for some salvation and sanity. It was from there she began truly experimenting with recipes and quickly learned she had the ability to get a little more creative in the kitchen and develop her own recipes.

In 2010, Hope started her blog, *A Busy Mom's Slow Cooker Adventures*, to simply share the recipes she was making with her family and friends. She never imagined people all over the world would begin visiting her page and sharing her recipes with others as well. In 2013, Hope self-published her first cookbook, *Slow Cooker Recipes 10 Ingredients or Less and Gluten-Free*, and then later wrote *The Gluten-Free Slow Cooker*.

Hope became the new brand ambassador and author of Fix-It and Forget-It in mid-2016. Since then, she has brought her excitement and creativeness to the Fix-It and Forget-It brand. Through Fix-It and Forget-It, she has written *Welcome Home Super Simple Entertaining, Fix-It and Forget-It Healthy Slow Cooker Cookbook, Forget-It Cooking for Two, Fix-It and Forget-It Instant Pot Cookbook, Fix-It and Forget-It Freezer Meals, Welcome Home Diabetic Cookbook,* and many more.

Hope lives in the city of Clinton Township, Michigan, near Metro Detroit. She has been happily married to her husband and best friend, Justin, since 2008. Together they have two children, Ella and Gavin, who are her motivation, inspiration, and heart. In her spare time, Hope enjoys traveling, singing, cooking, reading books, spending time with friends and family, and relaxing.